*Feel good
with healthy
crave-worthy
recipes*

dig in
for the love of food

FALL IN LOVE WITH EATING NUTRITIOUS AND CRAVE-WORTHY FOODS

THAT FEED AND FUEL YOUR BODY.

Dig In by Chef Karla Angel

Recipes and text © 2023 by Karla Angel | Chef Karla LLC, chef-karla.com
Photography ©2023 by Rob Kaufman | Kaufman Photography, kaufmanphotography.com
Design ©2023 by Cindy Hooker | Cyd Consulting Ltd, hellocyd.com

Hilton Head Island, South Carolina
chef-karla.com | karla@chef-karla.com

contents

dig in
for the love of food

FALL IN LOVE WITH NUTRITIOUS AND CRAVE-WORTHY FOODS THAT FEED AND FUEL YOUR BODY.

Life is all about digging in. Especially good food! Dig into your food, fitness, faith, family, friends, and goals, embracing it all. Why do anything that you aren't all-in on?

The terms "wellness," "healthy," "diet," and "cleanse" all suggest eating less. I think we should flip the script in a culture where food restriction is celebrated. Let's dig into healthy, flavorful, colorful, bold food! Food is fuel, my friends, and food is ah-mazing! Proper nutrition can improve your sleep, mood, overall health, skin, and athletic performance, just to name a few benefits.

We have been told that you should eat less if you want to lose weight. However, optimum health requires

food! You must balance your nutritional needs so that your body can perform in the gym, sustain energy throughout your workday, and support healthy hormone function to burn excess body fat. When you properly fuel your body, your wellness goals, whatever they may be, are much easier to achieve.

This book is for you if you want to lose weight, increase athletic performance, elevate your nutrition, be inspired in the kitchen, or support healthy hormones.

This book is created to help feed and fuel your body, with your family, friends, and food cravings in mind.

my story

My love of food started at a young age.

As a busy athletic teenager raised by my father, I began my wellness journey. I cringe when I think about what I ate every day. While I was learning to prepare dinners for my dad and me, my daily lunch could have been healthier. Whether it was game day or not, my lunch was a giant M&M cookie, curly fries, and a Mt. Dew! Yikes! My soccer coach made the entire team give up drinking soda during the season. So just like that, lunch became a giant M&M cookie, curly fries, and water. The coach ignited one small change. From then on, I rarely drank soda and started carrying a water bottle everywhere. While my diet left a lot to be desired, I began to see the correlation between my food intake and my athletic performance.

My curiosity continued as I started experimenting in the kitchen, consuming the Food Network and every cookbook I could get my hands on. I did make a lot of terrible food, but I also learned a lot. It was the perfect storm; the need to prepare meals for my Dad and me and the desire to perform athletically. The combination led me to jump into creating healthy crave-worthy food and choosing to follow this wellness path.

I went on to receive a Bachelor's in Nutrition Science and an Associate's in Culinary Arts. Then I learned many tricks of the trade working as an executive chef at a wellness resort, a traveling private chef, and a chef consultant. I now love sharing how to bring food to life through fresh ingredients, bold flavors, and classic cooking techniques in simple everyday recipes. Packing in more nutrition by loading up on fresh produce wherever possible, more fiber, and more nourishing ingredients, creating delicious-tasting food that is good for you. If you can enjoy the process and the results you are more likely to stick to the steps you take toward a healthier lifestyle. When it comes to health and nutrition, starting small is where the magic is. When it comes to a lasting healthy lifestyle, research shows you're better off making small, consistent changes rather than aiming for a major diet or lifestyle overhaul.

Wherever you are in your wellness journey, simple and approachable changes can create a life of sustainability, overall health, and enjoyment. Please don't rush the process; enjoy it and dig in.

balance

It's all about balance!

A healthy diet can allow room for your favorite foods and treats.

What does balance look like?

It's different for everyone. Everybody has their favorite foods, food cravings, family traditions, etc. In addition, everyone has varied nutrient and caloric needs. So, what works for one person may not be your jam. The simplest way to look at balanced nutrition is one meal at a time. As you build your plate, aim to fill half with vegetables, one-fourth with protein, and one-fourth with a carbohydrate source. If your meal generally needs sauce or dressing, 1-2 tablespoons is adequate. Aim to build your snacks in a healthy format as well. When possible, include fruits and vegetables and pair them with healthy fat and/or protein. All the book's recipes have been developed around this balanced nutrition format.

Sparingly feel free to enjoy and indulge in your favorite treats. However, as you prioritize these healthier meals and build healthy, filling, and satisfying plates, the cravings and desires for highly palatable and low nutrient foods become fewer.

Remember, food is fuel, and food is meant to be enjoyed. To ensure you consume loads of goodness from what you eat, aim to eat a balanced variety of food groups because they are all gems in their own right.

the gems

Macronutrients

Macronutrients are just that, nutrients that the body requires the largest amounts of to be consumed. Carbohydrates, fats, and proteins are macronutrients. Tracking macronutrients has become a popular and effective tool for eating well. Balancing the proper portions of macronutrients daily can impact overall body composition and align you with your performance goals.

Carbohydrates

Carbohydrates have unfairly been given a bad reputation. They can make our souls sing and feel satisfied, energetic, and happy. Our bodies need carbohydrates as they are the body's preferred energy source. Carbohydrates fuel our bodies with the energy needed to move throughout the day, perform in the gym, and fuel our organs to function.

Where does this bad reputation stem from, then? Most likely, we can thank carbohydrates, evil twin, simple carbohydrates. Simple carbs include white pasta, rice, white bread, and sugary processed foods or drinks. Simple carbohydrates are high in sugar and provide litte to no nutrient value. They elevate the blood sugar quickly, then leave it to drop quickly, which can lead to feeling sluggish and hungry.

The best forms of carbohydrates are complex carbohydrates. Complex carbohydrates require more time and energy to digest, which means they will keep us fuller longer and are high in nutrients like fiber, protein, vitamins, and minerals. Due to the additional protein and fiber, complex carbohydrates do not cause a spike in blood sugar like their evil twin, simple carbohydrates. Examples of great complex carbohydrates include:

• Starchy vegetables: carrots, sweet potatoes, potatoes, butternut squash

• Beans

• Whole grain products: bread, tortillas, pasta

• Whole grains: quinoa, brown rice, farro, barley

Generally, 40% of your caloric intake should be carbohydrates. For example, if your daily caloric intake is 2,000 calories, you should consume about 200 grams of carbohydrates daily.

Proteins

Protein is mighty indeed! Protein is famous for building those bulging biceps, standing up that heavy back squat, and holding you upright all day long. Yet, it also creates satiety, supports and builds muscle mass, and repairs, grows, and reproduces cells.

Protein is found throughout your body, in muscle, bone, skin, hair, and virtually every other body part or tissue. It makes up the enzymes that power many chemical reactions. As the body digests protein, it converts it into amino acids, also known as "building blocks." Protein is made up of 20 different amino acids.

Amino acids are categorized into three groups:

• Essential: Cannot be made by the body and must be supplied by food. There are 9 essential amino acids.

• Non-essential: Are made by the body from essential amino acids or in the normal breakdown of protein.

• Conditional: Needed in times of illness or stress.

Healthy protein choices are key. When we eat foods for protein content, consider the other nutrients that come along with it; sodium, saturated fat, fiber, etc.

Aim to choose healthier proteins such as:

• Seafood
• Chicken and turkey breast
• Legumes and beans
• Nuts and seeds
• Grass-fed and pasture raised eggs
• Grass-fed red meat
• Milk, Greek yogurt, cottage cheese
• Whole grains (oats, farro, quinoa)

There's a wide range of acceptable protein intake, ranging from 10%-35% of caloric intake depending on lifestyle. For example, if your caloric intake is 2,000, you could consume 50 grams-175 grams of protein daily. Vegetarians and vegans will likely be on the lower end.

Fats

Let's bust the myth right away, fat is essential, and fat is good for you! It is not the enemy as it once was portrayed. Not only is fat good for you and necessary, but it's also delicious! Fat adds viscosity and texture to food.

Fat regulates body temperature, produces hormones, protects vital organs, and provides energy. Specific vitamins can only be absorbed in the presence of fat, vitamins A, D, E, and K. These vitamins are fat-soluble. For example, suppose you cook your eggs in a little olive oil for breakfast. Your body can absorb the vitamin A in the egg yolk more quickly due to the olive oil consumed alongside it. Also, fat is responsible for providing

our body with essential fatty acids such as omega-3 fatty acids. Omega fatty acids reduce inflammation and promote heart health. To ensure you consume optimum omega-3 fatty acids, eat salmon 2-3 times per week.

What we need to know about fat is that it is a calorically dense macronutrient. Meaning it provides a higher caloric count per gram than carbohydrates and protein. Specifically, fat provides 9 calories per gram, while carbohydrates and fat provide 4 calories per gram. Another valuable takeaway when discussing fat is that there are good forms of fat, and forms of fat that should be limited.

Healthy Fats

Unsaturated fats (liquid at room temperature):

• Olive oil, nuts, avocado oil, seeds

Some saturated fats (solid at room temperature):

• Whole food sources: Coconut oil, grass-fed butter, grass-fed meats, organic dairy products

Omega 3 fatty acids:

• Salmon, grass-fed and pasture-raised meats, eggs, flax seeds, chia seeds, mackerel, sardines

Unhealthy Fats

Partially hydrogenated oils, damaged/oxidized fats, and trans-fatty acids including;

• Canola oil, sunflower oil, corn oil, cottonseed oil, grapeseed oil, and soybean oil.

• Found in processed foods, snack foods (chips, cookies, crackers), some salad dressings, fried foods, coffee creamers, peanut butter (swap your peanut butter for natural to avoid this unnecessary addition.)

Generally, 30% of your caloric intake should be fat. For example, if your daily caloric intake is 2,000 calories, you should consume about 67 grams of fat daily.

A good takeaway regarding fat is to consume it in moderation and choose healthy forms. When purchasing food products, read the nutrition label and ingredient list to make informed decisions.

dig in to what matters most

Quality whole foods

Focusing on consuming more quality whole food sources is a simple yet, effective way to elevate your nutrition. Think about crowding out processed foods with more whole foods. Often, choosing more fruits, vegetables, whole grains, healthy proteins, and nuts seems much more straightforward and more sustainable than thinking, "I should avoid chips, pasta, cookies, and some of my favorite treats."

Whole foods provide far more nutrients than processed foods. The bounty of vitamins and minerals in fruits and vegetables is incredibly beneficial to your body. Vitamins and minerals are categorized as micronutrients. Micronutrients are often overlooked in health and wellness. However, they are necessary for our health. Micronutrients are vitamins and minerals that the body requires smaller amounts of these nutrients.

Vitamins perform hundreds of essential roles in the body. These under-celebrated rock stars convert food into energy, boost and support immune function, repair cellular damage, and support blood clotting. For example, niacin, also known as Vitamin B3, is an enzyme needed for energy metabolism, essential for nervous system support, proper digestion, and skin health. Excellent food sources of niacin include whole grains, leafy greens, mushrooms, and asparagus.

Another critical topic overlooked in healthy diets is minerals. Minerals are also under-celebrated yet incredibly essential to assist our bodies in performing hundreds of functions. Sodium, potassium, zinc, calcium, and magnesium are just a few. For example, potassium is a mineral that your cells, nerves, and muscles need to function correctly. Have you ever had a charley horse? Ouch! Eating a banana is the simple remedy for a charley horse and muscle cramping. That is because of the hefty amount of potassium a banana packs.

Eating a diet rich in fruits, vegetables, healthy proteins, whole grains, nuts, and seeds will provide your body with adequate vitamins and minerals to achieve these necessary functions for optimum health. The Standard American Diet (SAD) is typically deficient in vitamins and minerals due to the convenience of overprocessed foods. When foods are processed and formed into highly palatable, convenient meals and treats, they are stripped of their vitamins and minerals.

This cookbook aims to provide you with a plethora of good-for-you, nutrient-dense, simple, and tasty recipes so you can maintain great health while juggling your busy demanding life.

Grazing is good

Have you ever been "hangry"? Hangry is a state of anger caused by a lack of food. Hangry is an actual symptom of skipping snacks or meals. Hunger causes a shift in hormones, brain processes, and the nervous system. Essentially, the brain is fueled by glucose, AKA carbohydrates. When it doesn't have the necessary glucose levels, the brain cannot filter emotions, including fear, anger, sadness, and anxiety.

To maintain excellent energy levels, a stable mood, and focus, eat balanced meals and snacks throughout the day. To stay at the top of your game, aim to eat balanced meals or snacks every 3-4 hours, depending on your daily activities and expenditure.

Hydration

Drinking filtered water has many benefits. Water regulates body temperature, rids the body of waste, promotes cardiovascular health, increases energy and brain function, and aids joint and muscle function. Aim to drink at least half of your body weight in ounces daily. For example: If you weigh 150 pounds, aim to drink at least 75 ounces daily. If you are active or live-in warmer climates leading you to sweat more, compensate for the fluid loss by drinking more water.

The best way to stay adequately hydrated is to make it easy.

- Carry a bottle of water around with you everywhere you go.

- Add fruit to your water to add flavor. For example, adding a pineapple core to your water bottle is a nice tropical treat.

- Have a glass of water with each meal and snack.

- Enjoy sparkling water for variety.

Sleep

It seems simple, yet sleep is often overlooked for contributing to good health. Sleep is a necessary process our bodies need to recover, grow, and heal properly. If necessary, prioritize sleep as though it's your job. Give it the attention it deserves. Create a routine around sleep and stick to it for at least 5-6 days of the week. Aim to sleep 7-9 hours each night.

Movement

Celebrate your capable body by moving it! Find what works for you. Everyone is on a different journey, and all fitness levels vary. The goal for your movement is to find something you enjoy, and that can fit into your lifestyle. Daily activity and exercise will strengthen your bones and muscles, improve sleep, create an endorphin release (happy hormone), improve stability and coordination, and aid in weight management. Make time for movement; briskly walk 2-3 times a day for 10 minutes, join a gym with a workout buddy, find a fitness class you enjoy, or join a local recreational team.

Consistency

The overall goal of including healthier practices in your life is to do them consistently. Our overall goal for our health is to feel good, perform well, be energetic, and enjoy our lives, right?

Are you familiar with the compound effect? The strategy of doing small things consistently will add up and create a more significant result. Healthy habits are the perfect canvas for the compound effect. Small changes over a long period create POWERFUL results. Eating one or two cookies will not ruin you and your health.

On the other hand, eating one kale salad will not give us everlasting health. What we do consistently will be the determining factor of our health. Find a good rhythm to your wellness and prioritize what is important to you. Balance your nutrition as best you can, and make healthier choices for your lifestyle, not a diet, not a fling; make it stick.

meal prepping

The key to eating healthier is being prepared. Whether you love to cook and spend time in your kitchen or loathe cooking, cooking takes valuable time from our already demanding schedules. When time is limited, we want the healthy option to be easy. Currently, the food industry has made the convenient option the unhealthy choice for the most part. Most convenience foods are higher in sugar, salt, unhealthy fats, empty calories, and served with minimal fresh produce.

Let's handle this and take control of our nutrition. The best fix is to meal plan. Everyone will have a different approach to meal planning and meal prepping. The first and most crucial step is to create a plan. Take a few minutes at the start of each week and jot down which recipes and meals you will make for the upcoming week (including snacks and breakfasts). Then, in the same setting, write out your grocery list. Be mindful of your upcoming week: if there are any late work nights, if someone in the household is out of town for a few days, etc. The idea here is to have a well-thought-out, stocked kitchen each week.

A fully stocked kitchen will hold us accountable and aid in skipping takeout when we know we can easily whip up a healthy meal. Next, this is when the approach varies for everyone. You can prep a few ingredients days in advance, make dinners/meals each night, have one or two big prep days, and prep all of the food for the week. Either way, find a groove that works for you and your schedule. Mix and match approaches if that works for you. The biggest goal here is to have a plan. We all eat three to five times each day. Let's plan accordingly!

Food storage

Let's make your food and meals work for you! The rule of thumb for food storage is that cooked food lasts 7 days in a sealed container in your fridge. The only exception to the rule is seafood. Seafood typically only lasts 1-3 days in the refrigerator once it's cooked. Seven days, that's a hefty amount of time, isn't it? Use that amount of time to your advantage. Bulk cooking and prepping will save you time. All food will last in your freezer for up to 6 months. I urge you to label everything you put into your freezer. Trust me, we all have that mystery container that will never be eaten. Nobody is that daring.

Freezer-friendly foods

Freezing prepped foods and meals is an awesome way to extend your meal prep, preserve meals from waste, and save time. You will be surprised; you can freeze more than you think.

Here are a few general rules when freezing foods:
1. Dairy Dislikes Freezing.
Items like the Green Goddess dressing will not freeze well because of the emulsified cottage cheese. When it thaws, the water will separate from it, and it won't be the gorgeous creamy dressing we love. It isn't dangerous, but it is just not tasty. It loses its quality. Think about freezing a pizza. The cheese is on top, not emulsified. The general rule is to avoid freezing creamy dressings, puddings, and sauces.
2. Allow Room for Expansion.
When freezing liquid items like soups, stocks, or vinaigrettes, they will need a bit more room in the container once they freeze as they will expand. We don't need the lids popping off and creating a mess.
3. Produce is Precious.
Fruits and vegetables are great to freeze. However, when they thaw, a lot of the water is released; thus, they lose their crunch. It's okay to freeze fresh fruits, and fresh vegetables, as well as cooked fruits and cooked vegetables When using frozen fresh or cooked produce, I recommend using them in something that will allow you to emulsify the produce. Make a roasted vegetable vinaigrette, fruit or vegetable smoothie, or savory soup.

Foods that freeze well:
- Pancakes
- Cooked and cooled whole grains: rice, quinoa, farro, barley, prepared oatmeal, etc...
- Prepared casseroles: lasagna, enchilada casserole, etc...
- Cooked and cooled pasta
- Egg bakes, quiches, or bites
- Cooked and cooled proteins: pulled pork tenderloin, grilled chicken, grilled turkey burgers
- Soups
- Chili and stews
- Meatloaf
- Sauces and vinaigrettes
- Energy bites
- Muffins and bread

recommended

Throughout the book, I make general references to many products. Here are my go-to food products in the kitchen. These items make preparing recipes more time effective, flavorful, and nutrient-dense.

Bread/English muffins/Burger buns
Dave's Killer Bread

Tortillas
Mission Carb Balance

Pancake mix
Kodiak
Birch Benders (Gluten free)

Pickled cabbage/Saurkraut
Wildbrine
Kraut

Naan bread
Stonefire

Hot sauce
Cholula

Protein powders
Ascent (Whey)
Active Stacks (Dairy-free)
Orgain (Plant-based)

Canned tomatoes
San Marzano

Marinara
Rao's
Primal Kitchen

Refried beans
Amy's
A Dozen Cousins
Siete
Eden

Buffalo wing sauce
Frank's Red Hot Wing

Pita bread
Joesph's pita
Stonefire

Verde salsa
Hernandez

Mayonnaise
Primal Kitchen

Gluten free all-purpose flour
Bob's Red Mill 1:1 Flour

Granola
Purely Elizabeth

Sweetener substitute
Truvia
Lakanto

Instant oatmeal
Better oats

Powdered peanut butter
PB2
PB Fit

BBQ sauce
Primal Kitchen

dedication

To Aaron.
My supportive husband. You are my number one taste-tester, dishwasher, and encourager. Thank you.

To my dad.
Whose encouragement inspired me to do what I love courageously.

In memory of Drexel Keith Williams, 1947-2018
The very best of Dads.

start your day

Good Morning! Breakfast is my favorite meal of the day. These recipes will have you jumping out of bed to start your day off right. In this chapter, you will find; quick and easy recipes, weekend brunch-friendly foods that pair perfectly with a mimosa, and meals you can make in advance for a grab-and-go morning. Each recipe is made with you and your health in mind, composed of whole foods, plenty of protein to keep you satisfied, and under 500 calories.

Breakfast

6 ways with toast
    Street corn salsa
    Roasted broccoli
    Lox & cream cheese
    Egg & avo
    Fuity yogurt
    Garlic hummus

Let's get smooth
    Sweet potato
    Island green
    Double chocolate cherry
    Carrot, citrus, & ginger
    Black magic

Feel your oats
    Overnight espresso chai
    Apple pie protein
    Samoa cookie
    Cranberry orange

Have an egg-cellent day
    Bacon & veggie quiche
    Ham, egg, & cheese breakfast sandwich
    Sundried tomato basil & egg cups
    Go-go breakfast burrito

Slow mornings
    Weekend fluffy pancakes
    Champion hash
    Blueberry muffins

V Vegetarian   VE Vegan   GF Gluten Free   DF Dairy Free

6 ways with toast

A healthy satisfying breakfast doesn't require heaps of prep and time. Start with toasted sourdough or whole wheat toast, a nice shmear of flavor, and build with healthy proteins and produce. Simply build a flavorful, nutrient-dense, and easy breakfast toast to begin your day.

Here are some of my favorite flavor combinations that come together in a snap.

Street corn salsa toast
with avocado

Serves 1 - Serving 1 assembled toast

1 slice Whole grain toast
½ each Avocado
¼ cup Street corn salad
  (see recipe page 54)

This is a fun take on the traditional avocado toast. Use your leftover street corn salad to whip-up a quick and healthy breakfast.

- Place mashed avocado on toasted bread.
- Top with street corn salad.
- Garnish with a squeeze of fresh lime juice.

Nutrition Note

Avocados are nutritious and versatile. These gorgeous fruits are rich in many nutrients that are often lacking in many people's diets; magnesium, vitamin C, vitamin E, and folate.

Calories: 310 | Fat: 17 grams | Carbs: 32 grams | Protein: 8 grams | Fiber: 12 grams

Roasted broccoli toast
with lemon ricotta spread

Serves 1 - Serving 1 assembled toast

Roasted broccoli

4 cups (12 oz) Broccoli florets
1 teaspoon Salt
1/2 teaspooon Ground black pepper
1 teaspoon Garlic powder
1 teaspoon Onion powder
1 teaspoon Olive oil

Lemon ricotta spread

1 each Lemon, zested, and wedges
1 tablespoon Olive oil, divided
4 slices Whole grain bread, toasted
¾ cup Ricotta cheese, part-skim
1/4 teaspoon Red pepper flakes
1 teaspoon Salt

Broccoli for breakfast? Let's do this! The crunchy char of broccoli florets in the morning paired with a sweet citrus ricotta spread, and crusty toast will make you swoon. You will love this non-traditional breakfast.

- Preheat the oven to 375 degrees F. Line a baking sheet with foil and spray with nonstick spray.
- In a mixing bowl combine; broccoli, salt, pepper, garlic powder, and onion powder.
- Spread out on a lined sheet tray.
- Roast for 12 minutes, or until the broccoli is golden brown and the tops of the florets are crispy.
- Place the ricotta cheese, olive oil, red pepper flakes, lemon zest, and salt in a food processor and blend until smooth and creamy.
- To assemble the toast, spread 3 tablespoons of ricotta cheese on toast. Top generously with the roasted broccoli. Sprinkle with crushed red pepper flakes. Serve with lemon wedges for spritzing.

Nutrition Note

There is nothing like getting a full serving of vegetables in as you start your day. Your body will thank you. Broccoli is a great source of fiber and many vitamins and minerals including vitamin C, calcium, and iron.

Calories: 315 | Fat: 15 grams | Carbs: 35 grams | Protein: 14 grams | Fiber: 10 grams

Lox & cream cheese toast

with onions , cucumbers, and capers

1 each Whole grain bread, toasted
2 tablespoons Cream cheese
2 ounces Smoked salmon, sliced
4-5 slices Cucumber
1 tablespoon Red onion, julienned
Small handful Arugula
2 teaspoon Capers

A classic, yet a staple. You don't have to leave your home to delight in this classic combination.

- Spread cream cheese on toast.
- Top with sliced cucumbers, smoked salmon, arugula, onion, and capers.

Nutrition Note

Jazz up this breakfast staple with the addition of arugula and cucumbers for flavor, crunch, and antioxidants. Additionally, salmon is a nutrient powerhouse, it is high in protein and omega-3 fatty acids, an essential fatty acid. It is bursting with potassium, vitamin D, and iron.

Calories: 280 | Fat: 13 grams | Carbs: 26 grams | Protein: 17 grams | Fiber: 5 grams

Egg & avo toast

with EBTBS, honey & pistachios

1 each Whole grain bread, toasted
1/2 each Avocado
1 teaspoon "Everything but the bagel" seasoning
1 each Egg, fried
1 teaspoon Pistachios, chopped
1/2 teaspoon Honey

Eggs and honey? It may seem like an odd combination, but I call it perfection. It's a flavor combination that is beyond good. Trust me on this one.

- Place sliced avocado on toast.
- Sprinkle with everything but the bagel seasoning.
- Top with fried egg, garnish with pistachios and honey.

Nutrition Note

Eggs are loaded with protein, selenium, and are a great whole food source of vitamin A.

Calories: 380 | Fat: 23 grams | Carbs: 35 grams | Protein: 14 grams | Fiber: 12 grams

Fruity yogurt toast

1 slice Whole grain bread, toasted
3 tablespoons Greek non-fat yogurt, vanilla
2 each Strawberries, sliced
½ each Kiwi, sliced
1 tablespoon Coconut flakes, toasted

Start your morning simply. It's a tasty classic combination of fruit and yogurt surfing on a nutrient-dense slice of bread.

- Spread yogurt onto toast.
- Top with kiwi, strawberries, and finish with toasted coconut.

Nutrition Note

This toast packs a big nutrition punch, the Greek yogurt contains protein and calcium and the fresh fruit provides vitamin C and potassium. Whole grain bread provides protein, fiber, and carbohydrates to support your busy day ahead.

Calories: 210 | Fat: 5 grams | Carbs: 35 grams | Protein: 10 grams | Fiber: 7 grams

Garlic hummus toast

with herbed mushrooms & balsamic

1 slice Whole grain bread, toasted
2 tablespoons Hummus
½ cup Mushrooms, sliced
2 tablespoons Balsamic vinegar
½ tablespoon Goat cheese, crumbled
1 teaspoon Nutritional yeast

This warm savory toast will hit the spot, it's layered with flavors and good-for-you ingredients. Feel free to use store-bought hummus to keep this recipe simple.

- Warm a sauté pan to medium-low heat. Add olive oil.
- Add sliced mushrooms and balsamic vinaigrette, and allow to sauté for 8-10 minutes until the balsamic has reduced and mushrooms have softened.
- Once mushrooms are cooked, build toast.
- Spread hummus on toast, top with balsamic mushrooms, sprinkle nutritional yeast, and finish with goat cheese.

Nutrition Note

Mushrooms are loaded with essential vitamins and minerals. These earthy gems contain selenium which supports good thyroid health.

Calories: 220 | Fat: 5 grams | Carbs: 35 grams | Protein: 9 grams | Fiber: 8 grams

Let's get smooth

Smoothies are awesome in many ways- quick and easy to make, delicious to drink, and they bump up your fruit and veggie intake for your day. If you are not much of a breakfast person smoothies can be a great way to ease into the day. Smoothies are also the perfect afternoon pick-me-up to keep you going until dinner.

Sweet potato smoothie

Serves 1 - Serving 1 assembled smoothie

1 each Roasted sweet potato, skin removed

1/3 cup Old fashion oats

2 cups Almond milk, unsweetened, vanilla

1 scoop (30 grams) Vanilla protein powder

1 ½ teaspoon Cinnamon, ground

¼ teaspoon Cloves, ground

¼ cup Riced cauliflower, frozen

For all the morning gym-goers, this healthy sweet potato smoothie is a great portable breakfast full of nutrients, protein, and flavor. It truly tastes like a sweet potato pie.

- In a blender, combine all ingredients.
- Blend until smooth.
- If it is too thick, add more almond milk until it reaches your desired consistency.

Nutrition Note

Sweet potatoes are packed with potassium, vitamin C, beta-carotene, and fiber. Talk about a superfood! Roast multiple sweet potatoes at a time, cool, remove the skin, and freeze for ease in whipping up your future smoothies.

Calories: 350 | Fat: 7 grams | Carbs: 50 grams | Protein: 27 grams | Fiber: 8 grams

Island green smoothie

Serves 1 - Serving 1 assembled smoothie

½ cup Spinach, fresh

1 cup Coconut water

1 cup Pineapple, frozen, diced

½ each Banana, ripe

½ cup Riced cauliflower

½ cup Greek non-fat yogurt, plain

Coconut and pineapple are the perfect disguises for sneaking spinach into a smoothie. If it weren't for the beautiful green color, nobody would notice this smoothie is packed with nutrient-dense spinach.

- In a blender combine ingredients.
- Blend until smooth.

Calories: 285 | Fat: 1 gram | Carbs: 54 grams | Protein: 18 grams | Fiber: 5 grams

Double chocolate cherry smoothie

1 scoop (30 grams) Chocolate protein
   powder
1 1/2 cups Almond milk, unsweetened,
   vanilla
3/4 cup Cherries, frozen
1/2 cup Cauliflower frozen
2 tablespoons Cocoa powder

Frozen cauliflower is a strong addition to this indulgent smoothie. It adds a nice thickness, takes the place of flavorless ice, and most importantly is great for helping your liver and kidneys detox. This smoothie is excellent for breakfast or a perfect post-workout snack.

- In a blender combine almond milk, cherries, and cauliflower. Blend well.
- Add protein powder and cocoa powder. Blend.
- If the smoothie is too thick, add more almond milk until it reaches your desired thickness.
- Store overnight in the fridge or drink immediately.

Calories: 265 | Fat: 7 grams | Carbs: 38 grams | Protein: 29 grams| Fiber: 11 grams

Carrot, citrus, & ginger smoothie

½ each Orange, peeled, seeds removed
½ inch nob/5 grams Ginger, fresh,
   peeled
½ inch nob/5 grams Turmeric, fresh,
   peeled
½ cup Carrots, peeled, chopped
1 cup Water
2 teaspoons Truvia
¼ teaspoon Black pepper

This smoothie is just what the doctor ordered. It's loaded with anti-inflammatory compounds, boosts immune function, and tastes refreshing. Turmeric absorbs more effectively when it is served with black pepper, don't skip this necessary ingredient.

- In a blender combine all ingredients.
- Blend until smooth.
- If it's too "pulpy" strain out and enjoy this flavorful combination as a juice.

Calories: 85 | Fat: .6 grams | Carbs: 20 grams | Protein: 2 grams| Fiber: 4 grams

Black magic smoothie

8 ounces Black coffee, cooled
1 scoop (30 grams) Chocolate protein
   powder
½ teaspoon Cinnamon, ground
1 tablespoon Coconut milk, canned
½ cup Cauliflower, riced, frozen

What makes this smoothie magic? You! The powerful combination of protein and caffeine makes you unstoppable! The protein content and fat aid in maintaining steady blood sugar levels while sipping on caffeine, avoiding that energy crash. Sip this tasty smoothie for a little boost of energy, nutrition, and magic.

- In a blender combine ingredients.
- Blend until smooth.

Calories: 140 | Fat: 3 grams | Carbs: 6 grams | Protein: 26 grams | Fiber: 2 grams

Feel your oats

Oatmeal is a classic breakfast, as it should be. Oats are a good source of complex carbohydrates and fiber. They are loaded with important vitamins and minerals including manganese, phosphorus, and zinc. In addition, oats contain good-for-you fiber which improves gut health, lowers LDL (bad) cholesterol levels, and keeps you fuller longer. Plus, oatmeal can be enjoyed in many ways; sweet, savory, warm, or cold there is an oatmeal out there for everyone!

Overnight espresso chai oats

Serves 4 - Serving 1 cup

1 cup Quinoa, cooked
1 cup Old fashion oats
¼ cup Maple syrup
1 ½ cups Milk, 2%
1 tablespoon Instant espresso powder
2 scoops (60 grams) Vanilla protein
  powder
1 teaspoon Cinnamon
1 teaspoon Cardamom
1 teaspoon Ground cloves
½ teaspoon Ginger, ground
½ teaspoon Black pepper, ground
¼ teaspoon Salt

Optional toppings
Greek vanilla yogurt
Cacao nibs
Fresh fruit
Almond butter
Granola
Shredded coconut

This bowl of overnight oats is the definition of a power breakfast! The small amount of espresso delivers a little caffeine and flavor, perfectly balanced with the sweet and savory delight of chai spice.

- In a microwave-safe bowl add milk. Microwave for 60-seconds or until warm.
- Add instant espresso to warmed milk, and stir.
- In a large storage container combine; quinoa, oats, maple syrup, protein powder, espresso milk mixture, and all spices.
- Stir until combined.
- Store in an airtight container in the refrigerator. This mixture can be eaten immediately or stored in the fridge for up to 7 days.
- To serve: scoop out 1 cup of mixture, warm for 45-seconds in the microwave, and top with your desired toppings.

Nutrition Note

Quinoa is an ancient grain, also considered a whole grain, yet technically a seed. Quinoa is a complete source of protein containing fiber, B vitamins, and antioxidants. Play around with the different toppings to build your perfect bowl. The yogurt will add more protein, fresh fruit will add to your antioxidant intake, and cacao nibs add great texture and welcomed earthy tones.

Calories: 270 | Fat: 5 | Carbs: 43 grams | Protein: 14 grams | Fiber: 5 grams

Apple pie protein oatmeal

Serves 1 - Serving 1 assembled bowl

1 packet Instant oatmeal
1/3 cup Egg whites
1/3 cup Milk, 2%
1 tablespoon Almond butter
1/4 cup Apple pie filling
(see recipe page 140))

This combination of oats, fruit, and almond butter elevates an instant oatmeal that whips up quickly yet, tastes as if simmered for hours.

- In a microwavable bowl, combine oats, egg whites, and milk.
- Microwave for 90 seconds, remove and stir.
- Continue to microwave oatmeal in 30-second intervals until desired consistency is reached.
- Top with fruit and almond butter.

Nutrition Note

Oatmeal is a complex carbohydrate, meaning it's slow-burning fuel, so an excellent way to begin the day. Oats also contain fiber, magnesium, and phosphorus. Mixing the oats with egg whites is an easy and different way to add more protein to your breakfast.

Calories: 360 | Fat: 13 grams | Carbs: 46 grams | Protein: 17 grams | Fiber: 4 grams

Cranberry orange oatmeal

Serves 6 - Serving 3/4 cup

2 cups Old fashion oats
3 cups Unsweetened vanilla almond milk
1/3 cup Flaxseeds, ground
2 teaspoons Cinnamon, ground
1/2 teaspoons Nutmeg, ground
1 tablespoon Vanilla extract
2 scoops (60 grams) Vanilla protein powder
1/2 cup Dried cranberries
1 tablespoon Orange zest

Garnish
6 tablespoons Pecans, chopped

As well as being quick and tasty this oatmeal gives us satiating protein and fiber. Ground flaxseeds contribute to nutrient density by contributing omega-3 fatty acids, which lower inflammation and LDL (bad) cholesterol.

- In a medium sauce pot over medium-low heat, combine, oats, milk, flaxseeds, cinnamon, nutmeg, and vanilla extract.
- Cook for 5-7 minutes, whisking occasionally.
- Remove from heat and stir in protein powder, cranberries, and zest.
- Garnish each serving with 1 tablespoon of pecans.

Note

Store oatmeal in an airtight container for up to 7 days in the refrigerator. Each morning, scoop out your portion, add a splash of milk to the bowl and, reheat, then top with pecans.

Calories: 300 | Fat: 12 grams | Carbs: 37 grams | Protein: 16 grams | Fiber: 9 grams

Samoa cookie oatmeal

2 cups Steel cut oats
1 can Full-fat coconut milk
5 cups Water
1 tablespoon Vanilla extract
1/4 cup Monk fruit sugar
1 tablespoon Coconut extract
1/2 cup Flax seeds, ground
2 cups Egg whites
1 teaspoon Salt

Caramel topping

1/2 cup Water, warmed
6 each Dates, pitted
1/2 tablespoon Vanilla extract
1/2 cup Shredded coconut flakes,
   unsweetened

Garnish

1/3 cup Chocolate chips

A new and much healthier take on my personal favorite Girl Scout cookie. Make this entire recipe and store it in your fridge for up to 7 days. Scoop out a portion each morning, add a splash of almond milk and reheat.

- In a slow cooker combine; oats, coconut milk, water, vanilla extract, and flax seeds.
- Turn the slow cooker on high heat and allow to cook for 4 hours, or until oats reached a creamy consistency.
- For the caramel topping, in a food processor combine, water, dates, and vanilla extract. Puree until smooth. Then add coconut flakes, and puree until just combined.
- Spoon out warm oatmeal in a bowl, top with 2 tablespoons of caramel topping and garnish with 2 teaspoons of chocolate chips.

Nutrition Note

Steel-cut oats are the least processed oats. They have even more protein, fiber, and micronutrients thus keeping us full until lunch and aiding in muscle growth and recovery.

Calories: 360 | Fat: 21 grams | Carbs: 29 grams | Protein: 12 grams | Fiber: 4 grams

Have an egg-cellent day!

Eggs are an egg-cellent way to start your day. Eggs are very nutrient-dense, whole eggs (yes, yolk included) contain protein, fat, choline, selenium, vitamin A, vitamin D, and vitamin B12.
Don't be scrambled by the media, eggs are a healthy breakfast staple and create a well-balanced breakfast.

Bacon & veggie quiche
with a sweet potato crust

Serves 6 - Serving 1/6 of quiche

Crust

2 Sweet potatoes, ~small, skin-on, ~400 grams
1 tablespoon Onion powder
1 tablespoon Garlic powder
2 teasoons Salt
1 teaspoon Ground black pepper
1 Egg

Filling

11 Eggs
1 1/2 cups Arugula
1/2 Red onion, diced
1 Bell pepper, diced
1 teaspoon Salt
1/2 teaspoon Ground black pepper
5 Bacon strips, cooked, chopped
1/4 cup Goat cheese, crumbled

Hugs and quiches! This sweet potato crust creates the perfect vehicle for our savory egg custard. Sweet potatoes lend a little sweetness to elevate the creamy savory filling, plus sweet potatoes add fiber, vitamin C, and beta-carotene.

- Preheat oven to 425 degrees.
- Rinse sweet potatoes and shred them. (The easiest and fastest way to shred is using your food processor with the shredder attachment, if you don't have that available, use a cheese grater.)
- Line the bottom of a springform pan or pie pan with a round of parchment paper. Lightly grease the pan using avocado oil spray. *If using a springform pan, wrap it in foil before baking. That way if the pan doesn't have a perfect seal, it won't make a mess in your oven.
- To make the crust, combine the shredded sweet potatoes, onion powder, garlic powder, salt, pepper, and egg. Mix well.
- Transfer shredded sweet potatoes to the pan, firmly and evenly press and spread the sweet potatoes out, creating a small edge up on the pan.
- Bake at 425 degrees for 20 minutes to set the crust. Once cooked, remove from oven, no need to cool crust prior to adding the filling.
- Drop oven temperature to 375 degrees.
- To make the filling; combine eggs, onion, bell peppers, salt, pepper, and bacon.
- Spread the arugula out on top of the prepared crust.
- Pour egg mixture on top of arugula, then crumble goat cheese on top of egg filling, evenly distributing the cheese.
- Bake for 45-60 minutes or until the center of the quiche is set.
- Serve warm or allow to cool and store in the refrigerator for up to 7 days.

Note

Serve a slice of this tasty quiche with a leafy green salad or fresh fruit, it's perfect for breakfast or lunch.

Calories: 250 | Fat: 14 grams | Carbs: 13 grams | Protein: 17 grams | Fiber: 2 grams

Ham, egg, & cheese breakfast sandwich

with raspberry jam

6 Whole wheat English muffin
6 tablespoons Raspberry jam
9 ounces Ham, sliced thin
6 slices Cheese, pepperjack
1 1/2 cups Spinach

Egg whites
2 cups Egg whites
1 tablespoon Everything but the bagel
    seasoning

There is something about eating a sandwich that feeds the soul, it is such a great way to start the day. The addition of the slightly sweet raspberry jam paired with a lightly spicy pepper jack cheese is the flavor combination you have been waiting for.

- Preheat oven to 350 degrees.
- To prepare the egg white cups, lightly grease a muffin pan or a silicone mold. Pour 1/3 cup of egg whites into 6 muffin cups.
- Sprinkle everything but the bagel seasoning on top of raw egg white cups.
- Bake for 16-18 minutes.
- Remove from oven and allow to cool.
- To build the sandwiches: Spread 1 tablespoon of jam on one side of the English muffin, and top with ham, then spinach, cheese, and cooked egg white cup, top with the other half of the English muffin.
- Wrap in aluminum foil. (Make all 6 at once for easy mornings!)
- Pop the wrapped sandwich in the oven for 20 minutes, or until the cheese is melted and the sandwich is warmed through.

Nutrition Note

This high-fiber English muffin, paired with protein-packed eggs and ham, are great ways to support our brain health, energy throughout the day, and muscle growth. Prepare enough for the entire week, wrap them individually in aluminum foil, and bake to reheat when you are ready to swoon over your breakfast.

Calories: 340 | Fat: 7 grams | Carbs: 40 grams | Protein: 22 grams | Fiber: 3 grams

Sundried tomato, basil, & egg cups

with feta cheese

4 cups Quinoa, cooked (about 1 1/2
 cups uncooked)
8 Eggs
1 cup Egg whites
2 1/2 cups Zucchini, shredded
6 ounces Feta cheese, crumbled
 (1 1/4 cups)
1 cup Parmesan cheese, shredded
1 cup Basil, fresh, chopped
1 cup Sundried tomatoes, sliced
1 bunch Green onion, minced
2 teaspoons Salt
1 teaspoon Ground black pepper

Protein, veggies, and whole grains, oh my! These flavorful egg cups are loaded with nutrition to start your day off fully energized and satisfied.

- Preheat oven to 350 degrees.
- Soak sundried tomatoes in warm water for 5 minutes.
- Combine all ingredients in a large bowl and mix to combine.
- Line a muffin tin with muffin liners.
- Scoop 1/4 cup of mixture into each muffin slot.
- Bake for 20 minutes, or until the edges of the cups are golden brown.
- Allow cooling for about 10 minutes before removing from the muffin pan.

Note

Get wild if you wish and add variety to this simple preparation by swapping different cheeses and vegetables for a new flavor. For ease, make ahead and store them in the fridge for up to 7 days, or freeze these cups for up to 6 months.

Calories: 345 | Fat: 15 grams | Carbs: 30 grams | Protein: 24 grams | Fiber: 5 grams

Go-go breakfast burrito

1 Bell pepper, small diced

1 Onion, small dice

1 teaspoon Olive oil

1 teaspoon Salt

1/2 teaspoon Ground black pepper

6 Eggs

2 cups Roasted potatoes

1 can Pinto beans, drained, rinsed
    (1 1/2 cups)

5 slices Bacon, cooked, chopped

1 cup Cheddar cheese, shredded

1/4 cup Cilantro

12 each Flour tortillas

A breakfast burrito that is good for you? Absolutely! Bell peppers contain vitamin C, while potatoes are high in potassium, and bacon is good for the soul. Pairing these with the nutrient-dense egg, and a fiber-filled tortilla creates a perfect breakfast burrito.

- In a large sauté pan, on medium heat, add oil.
- Add diced onions and peppers. Sauté, until lightly caramelized, about 4-5 minutes, stirring occasionally.
- In a bowl, crack eggs, and whip. Stir in salt and pepper.
- To the sauté pan, add roasted potatoes and pinto beans. Cook until warmed, about 4-5 more minutes.
- Add whipped eggs to sauté pan. Using a spatula scramble eggs in the pan and combine with the ingredients. Cook until eggs are done, about 3-4 minutes.
- Turn heat off and add bacon, cheddar, and cilantro, combine.
- Warm tortillas by placing them on a microwave-safe dish, cover them with a damp cloth or paper towel, and microwave for 30-seconds.
- Fill each warm tortilla with 1/2 cup of filling, wrap up, and enjoy.

Note

These breakfast burritos are perfect to take on the go! Ahead of time, make the filling, and build your burritos, and store in the fridge for up to 7 days. Wrap burritos in a damp paper towel and microwave for 45 seconds to 1 minute to reheat and go.

Calories: 470 | Fat: 20 grams | Carbs: 50 grams | Protein: 32 grams| Fiber: 16 grams

Slow mornings

I love a slow morning, waking up without an alarm clock, skipping the morning hustle, and the smell of freshly brewed coffee. It's the simple things in life, and a slow morning is at the top of my list. So these recipes were created for you to enjoy your leisurely start while keeping your nutrition and taste buds in mind.

Weekend fluffy pancakes

with strawberry syrup

Serves 5- Serving 1 pancake

1 1/4 cup Protein pancake mix
1/2 cup Egg whites
1/2 cup Greek non-fat yogurt
1/2 cup Milk, 2%
1/4 teaspoon Salt
1/4 teaspoon Ground cinnamon
1/4 cup strawberry syrup
   (see recipe page 92)

These pancakes are a great source of protein. Protein will help build and repair your muscles, thus making all your gym time count. Top these gorgeous pillows with a smear of almond butter and a maple syrup drizzle or with the strawberry syrup.

- In a medium mixing bowl, combine; egg whites, yogurt, and milk, and mix well.
- Add pancake mix, salt, and cinnamon.
- Preheat a medium-size sauté pan on medium-low heat.
- Lightly spray a pan with non-stick spray (avocado oil is excellent here).
- Pour a 1/2 cup of batter into a warmed pan.
- Allow bubbles to form on top of the pancake, then flip. It takes about 1-2 minutes on each side.
- Repeat until all of the batter is used. Drizzle with prepared strawberry syrup.

Note

Whip up a big batch and freeze for ease. Then, simply, reheat in the microwave.

Calories: 150 | Fat: 1 gram | Carbs: 24 grams | Protein: 10 grams| Fiber: 4 grams

Champion hash

with sweet potatoes and apples

GF DF

1 tablespoon Olive oil
5 each Chicken sausage, diced or
    removed from casing
3 each Bell peppers, diced
3 each Apples, diced, skin-on
2 each Sweet potato, diced, skin-on
1 each Onion, yellow, diced
1/2 teaspoon Salt
1/4 teaspoon Ground black pepper
10 Eggs

You are a champ - it's time to eat like one.

- Preheat oven to 400 degrees.
- Toss diced sweet potatoes with a 1/2 tablespoon of oil, a pinch of salt, and pepper.
- Lightly grease a sheet tray, and spread diced, seasoned potatoes onto the sheet tray.
- Roast sweet potatoes for 20-30 minutes or until fork tender.
- In a large sauté pan, add remaining oil (1/2 tablespoon), on medium heat.
- Add bell pepper, onions, and chicken sausage (raw). Sauté for 4-5 minutes, until onions caramelize and soften.
- Add roasted sweet potatoes and apples. Allow searing, only stirring about every 3-4 minutes. Cook until chicken sausage cooks through and apples are al dente.
- Lower temperature to medium-low heat. Crack eggs on top of hash and cover with lid. Allow to steam for 3-5 minutes or until eggs are cooked to your liking. *If you are prepping this hash ahead, skip adding the eggs, add them when you reheat.

Nutrition Note

This hash is loaded with whole foods, delivering the highest nutrition. Sweet potatoes, apples, bell peppers, and onions are full of fiber, potassium, and vitamin C, thus improving gut, brain, and immunity health.

Calories: 435 | Fat: 19 grams | Carbs: 38 grams | Protein: 31 grams | Fiber: 7 grams

Blueberry muffins

with almond flour & bananas

3 cups Almond flour
1/2 teaspoon Salt
1 ½ teaspoon Baking soda
2 tablespoons Coconut oil
1 tablespoons Vanilla extract
1/2 cup Flaxseeds, ground
4 Eggs
1 ½ cups (1 pint) Blueberries
4 Bananas, ripened

These gorgeous muffins are full of nourishing ingredients. Prepared with almond flour, coconut oil, sweetened with bananas, and topped with seasonally sweet blueberries.

- In a food processor, blend bananas until smooth.
- Add; almond flour, salt, baking soda, coconut oil, ground flax, and eggs. Blend until smooth.
- Fold in ½ of the blueberries into the batter.
- Scoop ¼ of a cup of batter into a lined muffin pan, and top each muffin batter with 5-7 blueberries, slightly pressing them in.
- Bake at 350 degrees for 25-30 minutes.

Note

This is your go-to recipe when you need to get rid of overripe bananas. Make a large batch and freeze.

Calories: 180 | Fat: 13 grams | Carbohydrates: 13 grams | Protein: 6 grams| Fiber: 4 grams

fuel throughout the day

All of your meals should be crave-able and satisfying. So whether you are taking your lunch on the go or sitting around the table with family for dinner, these recipes have you taken care of. This chapter is compiled of recipes that can be made in advance or whipped up in under 30 minutes. All of these recipes will be perfect for either lunch or dinner. Each recipe is loaded with flavor, good-for-you ingredients, and 500 calories or less.

Entrees

Salads
Salmon sushi bowl
Cranberry, walnut, & apple chicken salad
Loaded burger salad
Roasted vegetable & grain salad
Green goddess salad
Thai grain salad
Street corn salad

Grab & go
Chicken enchilada sliders
Southwest chicken crunch wrap
Chicken, bacon, & avocado wrap

One pot wonder
Slow cooker three bean chipotle chili
Egg roll in a bowl
Chipotle enchilada casserole
Creamy pesto chicken sausage pasta bake
Roasted vegetable & beef lasagna

A twist on the classics
Crispy fish tacos
Crispy baked chicken wings
Tostadas
Soul good loaded nachos
Spicy steak sheet-tray fajitas
Healthy burritos
Buffalo chicken stuffed sweet potato
BBQ chicken pizza
Zucchini & herb turkey burgers

Simple seafood
Mediterranean salmon en papillote
Miso peanut shrimp
Chili rubbed salmon

Working smart
Lemon dijon marinated chicken
Smoky verde pulled pork tenderloin
Simple taco meat

Vegetarian Vegan Gluten Free Dairy Free

Salads

Salads shouldn't be lame, lack creativity, nor "leaf" you feeling unsatisfied. Let's rewrite salad's role in this world, making them flavorful, full of different textures, and, you guessed it crave-worthy!

Salads can be an excellent entrée option or used as a side to elevate and round out your meal. It's up to you! The more flavor, texture, and variety you add equates to more nutrition and satisfaction.

Salmon sushi bowl

Serves 1 - Serving 1 bowl

4 ounces Salmon

1 teaspoon Avocado oil

1/4 teaspoon Salt

1/8 teaspoon Ground black pepper

1/2 cup Steamed coconut rice
  (see recipe page 104)

1/4 cup Arugula

1/4 cup Carrots, shredded

1/4 cup Cucumbers, diced

2 tablespoons Green onion, sliced

2 tablespoons Red beet and cabbage
  kraut

2 tablespoons Miso peanut sauce
  (see recipe page 94)

Craving sushi? This dish will satisfy your hunger. Think of it as a deconstructed sushi roll, but better. It's a great filling meal.

- Preheat oven to 400°F. Preheat a sauté pan to medium-high heat. Add oil.
- Add salmon to the pan, and sear on each side for 3-4 minutes or until nice and crispy (Once you place the salmon in the pan, don't touch it until it's ready to be flipped). Place salmon on an oven safe pan and finish baking in the oven for 4-5 minutes or until the internal temperature reaches 140°F. (While it rests outside of the oven, the salmon will carryover cook to 145°F., the optimum temperature for seafood.)
- Meanwhile, build your bowl. Place warmed coconut rice in the bottom of a serving bowl, add a bundle of arugula, handful of carrots, and when salmon is perfectly cooked, place it on top of veggies and rice, drizzle prepared miso peanut sauce, and garnish with green onion.

Nutrition Note

Salmon is rich in omega-3 fatty acids, an essential fatty acid. Omega-3 fatty acids reduce inflammation and lower blood pressure. Salmon is an excellent source of vitamins and minerals, including vitamin A (eye health), vitamin D, and selenium (thyroid hormone metabolism). For adequate omega-3 intake, according to the American Heart Association, aim to consume at least two servings of salmon per week.

Calories: 475 | Fat: 20 grams | Carbs: 38 grams | Protein: 34 grams | Fiber: 5 grams

Cranberry, walnut, & apple chicken salad

1 1/2 pounds Chicken breast, cooked
1 Red onion, diced
3 Apples, medium, diced, skin-on
1 cup Celery, diced
16 ounces Cottage cheese, 4%
2 tablespoon Onion powder
6 tablespoon Dijon mustard
6 tablespoon Apple cider vinegar
1 teaspoon Salt
½ teaspoon Ground black pepper
1 cup Cranberries, dried
1 cup Walnuts, chopped

This combination is classic. Cranberries, walnuts, apples, onions, and celery tossed in a creamy dressing. The dressing base is made with protein-packed pureed cottage cheese, rather than mayonnaise. Trust me here; the cottage cheese is the perfect adjustment to this tasty classic.

- To make dressing; combine cottage cheese, onion powder, Dijon, vinegar, salt, and pepper in a food processor. Blend until combined and the cottage cheese is completely smooth.
- Shred cooked chicken breast. **Trick** Place in stand mixer bowl; use the paddle attachment on medium speed. Magic, shredded chicken!
- In a large bowl, combine; dressing, shredded chicken, onion, celery, apples, cranberries, and walnuts.

Note

To prepare chicken, bake, boil, pressure cook, or purchase rotisserie chicken. Serve this as a sandwich, on a bed of greens as a salad, or as a snack with crackers. This salad will keep in your fridge for up to 7 days.

Calories: 290 | Fat: 10 grams | Carbs: 22 grams | Protein: 26 grams | Fiber: 3 grams

Roasted vegetable & grain salad

tossed in a basil pesto vinaigrette

¾ cup Farro, raw
3 ½ cups Water
2 tablespoons Goat cheese, crumbled
¼ cup Basil pesto vinaigrette,
 (see recipe page 98)

Roasted vegetables
4 cups Vegetables diced; zucchini,
 yellow squash, onion
1 tablespoon Olive oil
¼ teaspoon Salt
¼ teaspoon Ground black pepper

We are breaking the rules! Not all salads need leaves. So let's roast our favorite vegetables, making them crispy and tender, toss them with a nutty grain, dress them with a punch of basil, and combine all that goodness with goat cheese! Yum!

- To prepare farro, combine farro and water in a medium saucepot. Bring to a boil. Once farro reaches a boil, turn the heat to low, and cover. Allow to steam for 17-20 minutes, or until farro has tripled in size.
- To roast the vegetables, preheat oven to 400 degrees.
- Combine diced vegetables with olive oil, salt, and pepper. Lightly grease a sheet tray with non-stick cooking spray. Spread seasoned vegetables evenly out on a tray. **Or start with 2 cups of roasted vegetables. Roast the vegetables for 30-40 minutes or until vegetables are caramelized.
- Remove vegetables from oven and combine with cooked farro, prepared basil pesto vinaigrette, and crumbled goat cheese.

Note

This salad will last in the refrigerator covered for up to 7 days. Make a large batch and enjoy it all week long. Top this gem with your favorite protein; sautéed chickpeas, seared chicken thighs, or a fresh catch. If you are starting with cooked farro and roasted vegetables, combine 2 cups of cooked farro and 2 cups of vegetables.

Calories: 275 | Fat: 11 grams | Carbs: 38 grams | Protein: 10 grams | Fiber: 5 grams

Loaded burger salad

with tomatoes, onions, bacon, & pickles

Burger meat

(Makes 8 servings)

1/2 tablespoon Avocado oil

1 pound Ground turkey breast

1 pound Ground beef, lean 90/10

2 tablespoons Onion powder

2 tablespoons Garlic powder

2 tablespoons Oregano, dried

1 teaspoon Red pepper flakes

1/4 cup Soy sauce

Salad goodies

(Makes 1 serving)

2 cups Spring mix

1/4 cup Cherry tomatoes, halved

2 tablespoons Red onion, sliced

1 slice Bacon, cooked, chopped

5 Pickles, sliced

2 tablespoons Honey Dijon vinaigrette
 (see recipe page 98)

1 Mini naan

Where are my burger fans? Salads have a bad reputation for being "rabbit food," and burgers have a bad reputation for being "unhealthy", but I love them both, let's just marry the two and have them live happily ever after.

- In a large sauté pan, on medium heat, add oil.
- Then add turkey breast and ground beef.
- As meat is cooking, continue to stir occasionally, breaking up the meat.
- Cook meat for 5-7 minutes.
- Then add the remaining seasonings; onion powder, garlic powder, oregano, pepper flakes, and soy sauce. Allow cooking until meat is fully cooked, stirring occasionally.

To build a salad

- Toss 2 cups of spring mix with two tablespoons of prepared honey dijon vinaigrette.
- Top the greens with 1/4 cup of tomatoes, two tablespoons of red onion, one slice of chopped bacon, five slices of pickles, and four ounces of warmed burger meat. Serve with toasted naan.

Nutrition Note

This burger salad is a great way to ramp up your vegetable intake for the day and enjoy the satisfying flavors of a burger.

Calories: 500 | Fat: 18 grams | Carbs: 43 grams | Protein: 38 grams | Fiber: 3 grams

Green goddess salad

with green goddess dressing

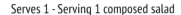

Serves 1 - Serving 1 composed salad

1 cup Broccoli slaw

1 cup Romaine, shredded

1/4 cup Edamame, shelled

1/4 cup Cucumbers, diced

1/4 Avocado, diced

1 Green onion, sliced

1 tablespoon Pistachios, chopped

2 tablespoons Green goddess dressing
  (see recipe page 96)

This bright, beautiful salad is just as tasty and satisfying as it looks. It is loaded with fresh green veggies and healthy fats and tossed in my all-time favorite dressing. The Green goddess salad has it all; looks, crunch, and creaminess.

- Combine all ingredients, and serve.

Nutrition Note

Broccoli slaw is an underrated ingredient, it is nutrient-dense and a great way to reduce food waste. Broccoli slaw is prepared using shredded broccoli stalks, and you can purchase broccoli slaw or prepare your own. Broccoli slaw is high in fiber, vitamins, minerals, and antioxidants. If you'd like, top this gorgeous salad with any additional protein; salmon, shrimp, chicken, or roasted garbanzo beans.

Calories: 210 | Fat: 10 grams | Carbs: 18 grams | Protein: 11 grams | Fiber: 8 grams

Thai grain salad
with miso peanut sauce

Farro
1 cup Farro, uncooked (3 cups cooked)
2 1/2 cups Water

Salad
1/2 cup Miso peanut sauce
  (see recipe page 94)
1 Bell pepper, diced
1/2 each Cucumber, diced
1 cup Pineapple, diced
1 cup Carrots, shredded
4 Green onion, sliced
1/2 cup Cilantro, minced
1 Jalapeno, seeded, minced

Farro is, hands-down, my favorite whole grain. It is popular in Mediterranean cuisine and gaining popularity due to its nice nutty flavor and a good hearty texture. Pairing farro with fresh crunchy vegetables, sweet pineapple, and tossing it in a peanut miso dressing makes whole grains cool again.

- In a medium saucepan, add farro and water, and bring to a boil. Once it comes to a boil, place a lid on top and turn the heat down to low. Allow to steam for 25-30 minutes or until the farro has tripled in size and is al dente. Pour off any excess water remaining.
- Once farro is perfectly cooked, set aside and allow to cool.
- Combine all ingredients in a large bowl.
- Serve warm or cold.

Nutrition Note
Farro is an excellent source of magnesium, zinc, iron, protein, and fiber. The Thai Grain Salad is perfect on its own or topped with seared salmon or chicken. You decide, either way, you will love it!

Calories: 160 | Fat: 2 grams | Carbs: 32 grams | Protein: 6 grams | Fiber: 4 grams

Street corn salad

with feta, cilantro, & jalapeno

Ⓥ ⒼⒻ

Serves 8 - Serving 1/2 cup

6 Ears of corn
1 cup Tomatoes, diced
½ each Red onion, diced
¼ cup Cilantro, chopped
¼ teaspoon Salt
¼ teaspoon Ground black pepper
3 tablespoons Lime juice, fresh
1 tablespoon Chili powder
¼ cup Feta cheese, crumbled
1 Jalapeno, seeds removed, diced

I love bringing this dish to a cookout or game night. It is easy to prepare, and it's a crowd-pleaser. Plus, it's incredibly versatile. You can serve it as a side salad, it's great on tacos, or use the leftovers on your breakfast toast in the morning.

- Preheat the grill. (If you don't want to fire up your grill, sauté the corn kernels in a sauté pan on medium-high heat with no added oil. Sauté until lightly charred.)
- Mark ears of corn on the grill, just until slightly charred, about 3-4 minutes, rotating occasionally.
- Remove corn from the grill. Once the corn is cooler to the touch, shuck corn kernels.
- In a bowl, combine; corn, tomatoes, red onion, cilantro, salt, pepper, lime juice, chili powder, feta, and jalapeno.
- Serve warm or cold.

Note

You can make this tasty salad in advance and serve it cold or serve it fresh off the grill.

Calories: 65 | Fat: 1 gram | Carbs: 2 grams | Protein: 1 gram | Fiber: 0 grams

Grab & go

Life can be busy, and we shouldn't have to sacrifice our nutrition or taste buds for our packed schedules. Having some grab-and-go options can be so helpful in keeping us fueled and energized throughout the day.

Chicken enchilada sliders
with chipotle enchilada sauce

Serves 6 - Serving 2 sliders

1 teaspoon Olive oil

1 Onion, diced

2 Garlic cloves, minced

12 ounces Shredded cooked chicken

1 ½ cups Chipotle enchilada sauce
  (see recipe page 94)

2 teaspoons Hot sauce

1/4 teaspoon Salt

1/8 teaspoon Ground black pepper

12 Slider buns

1 ½ cups Shredded cheddar

2 Green onion, sliced

2 tablespoons Butter, melted

The incredible classic flavors of chicken enchiladas served in cute sandwich form.

- Preheat oven to 350°F. In a large sauté pan over medium heat, add oil. Add onion and garlic and cook, occasionally stirring, until softened, about 5 minutes.
- Add shredded chicken, enchilada sauce, and hot sauce. Increase heat to medium-high and cook, stirring, until heated through, about 3 minutes. Season with salt and pepper. Remove from heat.
- Place the bottom half of the slider buns on a large baking sheet. Top the bottom half of the buns with prepared chicken, then cheddar, and green onions. Place the top buns on top and brush with melted butter.
- Bake until buns are golden and the cheese is melted, about 10 minutes.

Note

The homemade chipotle enchilada sauce elevates these sliders. Serve with a side salad or roasted bell peppers and onions, and maybe a margarita if it's that kind of evening.

Calories: 470 | Fat: 20 grams | Carbs: 41 grams | Protein: 32 grams | Fiber: 2 grams

Southwest chicken crunch wrap

with Jalapeno cilantro dressing

2 pounds Chicken, cooked

1 1/2 cups Corn, fresh or frozen

1 Red onion, diced

2 Bell peppers, diced

1 cup Cilantro, chopped

15 ounce can Black beans, drained, rinsed

1/2 cup Shredded cheddar

1/2 tablespoon Salt

24 Flour tortillas

2 cups Jalapeno cilantro dressing
(see recipe page 98)

This is my version of a more "responsible" quesadilla. It is loaded with healthy protein and veggies, yet it's tossed with a creamy sauce and cheese, then seared. That cheese and a nice sear, it just feeds the soul.

- In a large mixing bowl, shred cooked chicken. (If you have access to a stand mixer, add chicken to the mixing bowl and shred with the paddle attachment.)
- In a large bowl, combine all ingredients except the tortillas.
- Once the chicken mixture is combined, divide 3/4 cup of chicken between 2 tortillas, and wrap it into a burrito.
- Sear filled tortillas on medium heat, searing tortillas on the seamed side and flip, cooking for about three minutes per side until toasted. Serve warm.

Note

Make this recipe ahead by preparing the filling with the dressing, then wrap it in the tortilla up to a day in advance. If you are taking this on the-go or are in a pinch for time, skip searing it and serve it cold.

Calories: 430 | Fat: 13 grams | Carbs: 42 grams | Protein: 48 grams| Fiber: 14 grams

Chicken, bacon, & avocado wrap

with ranch dressing

4 ounces Chicken, cooked

2 Bacon, slices, cooked

1 Flour tortillas

1/4 Avocado, mashed

2 tablespoons Healthy ranch dressing
   (see recipe page 96)

1/2 cup Spring mix

1 Roma tomato, quartered

2 tablespoons Red onion, diced

Yum! This wrap is such a classic and necessary flavor combination. Creamy avocado paired with crispy bacon, smeared with zesty ranch dressing, and fresh crunchy vegetables.

- On a microwave-safe plate, place tortillas, and top with a damp paper towel. Microwave for :20 seconds, just until warm and pliable.
- Build wraps: mash avocado onto a tortilla, then add warmed chicken, tomato, onion, spring mix, bacon, and drizzle with ranch dressing.
- Wrap the tortilla up and enjoy!

Note

The lemon dijon marinated chicken recipe is great for this recipe. Or if you are limited on time, grab a rotisserie chicken or any leftover cooked chicken you have. This is an awesome wrap to take on the go, make this up to one day in advance.

Calories: 450 | Fat: 19 grams | Carbs: 21 grams | Protein: 52 grams | Fiber: 9 grams

One pot wonder

These one-pot wonders gain popularity thanks to their easy clean-up and family-pleasing tune. Quickly, reaching the "top hits" charts in all busy homes.

Prepare these meals ahead of time and serve on a busy weeknight or for an easy, low-maintenance weekend.

Slow cooker three bean chipotle chili

Serves 12 - Serving 1 1/2 cups

1-pound Turkey breast, ground
1-pound Ground beef, 90/10
2 tablespoons Olive oil
2 Onions, small diced
2 Bell peppers, small diced
20 ounces Cauliflower, riced, frozen
¼ cup Garlic, minced
2 Jalapeno, seeded, minced
56 ounces Crushed tomatoes, canned
4 tablespoons Chili powder
2 tablespoons Cumin
2 tablespoons Cocoa powder
¼ cup Chipotle peppers in adobo, minced
2 cups Black beans, drained, rinsed
2 cups Garbanzo beans, drained, rinsed
2 cups Pinto beans, drained, rinsed
2 teaspoons Salt

Everybody needs a go-to chili recipe. Nothing beats snuggling up with a great bowl of chili on cool Fall evenings, rainy days, and at football parties. This one will quickly become your favorite, chipotle in adobo peppers add warmth, while our secret ingredient, the cocoa powder, adds an unexpected depth of flavor.

- Combine all ingredients in a slow cooker.
- Turn on low to cook for 8-12 hours or on high for 6-8 hours.
- Stir occasionally throughout the cooking process.
- That's it. Top it with your favorite chili garnishes; avocado, sour cream, green onions, and dig in.

Note

This recipe creates a big batch. Separate what you need for the upcoming week and freeze the rest. The chili will store in the freezer for up to 6 months. I love to make this chili in my instant pot too. If you have one, I highly recommend it. Combine all ingredients, and cook on high pressure, sealed for 1 hour. Once cooked, release pressure, and serve.

Calories: 380 | Fat: 10 grams | Carbs: 42 grams | Protein: 31 grams | Fiber: 11 grams

Egg roll in a bowl

with coconut rice

DF

1 teaspoon Sesame oil

5 Chicken sausage links, removed from casing

1 bag Shredded cabbage/coleslaw mix (10-14 ounces)

1 tablespoon Garlic, minced

2 tablespoons Ginger, minced

3 Green onion, sliced

1 Bell pepper, diced

1 cup Carrots, shredded

¼ cup Cilantro, chopped

¼ teaspoon Red pepper flakes

3 tablespoons Low-sodium soy sauce

Inspired by tasty takeout eggrolls, this dish comes together in minutes. It's incredibly easy and a great weeknight meal. Serve with rice or quinoa to make a nicely balanced meal.

- Preheat a large sauté pan to medium heat.
- Add sesame oil.
- Add chicken sausage, garlic, and ginger. As it is cooking, break the meat up.
- Allow to cook for 5-7 minutes. Add bell pepper, green onion, and carrots.
- Continue to cook for about 5 minutes, allowing vegetables to caramelize.
- Add the bag of cabbage and soy sauce.
- Cook until the cabbage is slightly wilted, or about 5 minutes.

Nutrition Note

The egg roll in a bowl is a vegetable and protein-packed meal. Cabbage is packed with micronutrients, including folate, vitamin C, and vitamin B6. This dish is high in fiber and powerful antioxidants fueling you to take on your day.

Calories: 280 | Fat: 12 grams | Carbs: 13 grams | Protein: 31 grams | Fiber: 5 grams

Chipotle enchilada casserole

with roasted vegetables

7 cups Vegetables for roasting, (Bell peppers, onions, jalapenos, or zucchini)

2 teaspoons Olive oil

1 teaspoon Salt

½ teaspoon Ground black pepper

15 ounce can Black beans, rinsed and drained

18 Corn tortillas, cut in half

2 ½ cups Chipotle enchilada sauce, *(see recipe page 94)* or use canned enchilada sauce

1 pound Smokey verde pulled pork tenderloin *(see recipe page 88)*

1 ½ cups Mozzarella cheese, shredded

1 cup Cilantro, chopped

Classic flavors of enchiladas layered with corn tortillas and pumped up with roasted vegetables make this meal a crowd-pleaser. The addition of roasted vegetables adds volume and nutrition to this dish.

Roasting vegetables *This step can be done ahead of time. *

- Preheat oven to 425˚F.
- Dice vegetables into medium size chunks.
- In a bowl, combine; diced vegetables, oil, salt, and pepper.
- Place vegetables on a lightly greased baking sheet.
- Roast in the oven for about 20-30 minutes or until caramelized.
- Remove from oven.

Build the casserole

- Heat oven to 400°F. Mist a 9×13-inch baking dish with cooking spray; set aside.
- In a large bowl, combine; roasted vegetables, black beans, and cilantro.
- In a separate bowl, combine pulled pork with 1 1/2 cups of prepared enchilada sauce.
- Pour 1 cup of enchilada sauce into the baking dish and spread until the bottom is evenly coated.
- Place a total of 6 halved tortillas on the bottom layer, slightly overlapping each and covering the enchilada sauce. (Layer it similar to fish scales.)
- Top evenly with 1/2 of the vegetable mixture, then top with 1/2 of the pork mixture.
- Repeat with another layer of tortillas, then the vegetable mixture, then the pork mixture.
- Followed by a final layer of tortillas and the remaining enchilada sauce.
- Lastly, top with cheese.
- Bake for 20-25 minutes or until the cheese is melted and slightly caramelized.
- Remove from the oven and serve warm.

Note

Make ahead if you'd like and store in the fridge for up to 7 days. Or bake, cut into portions, and freeze portions for up to 6 months. Serve with shredded iceberg, avocado, and a drizzle of your favorite hot sauce.

Calories: 355 | Fat: 11 grams | Carbs: 40 grams | Protein: 27 grams | Fiber: 8 grams

Creamy pesto chicken sausage pasta bake

Serves 7 - Serving 1 1/2 cups

1 pound Chicken sausage links, casing removed

½ tablespoon Olive oil

7 cups Vegetables, diced (eggplant, zucchini, onion, peppers)

2 teaspoons Italian seasoning

½ teaspoon Ground black pepper

½ cup White wine

1 pound Whole wheat pasta, uncooked

Pesto

2 cups Basil, fresh (packed or 6 oz. basil)

10 Garlic cloves

3 teaspoons Salt, divided

¼ cup Parmesan cheese, shredded

1 ½ cups Cottage cheese, 4%

Topping

½ cup Panko breadcrumbs

½ cup Parmesan cheese, shredded

We are using whole wheat pasta in this recipe to bump up the protein and fiber amount. Plus, we loaded this dish with flavorful roasted vegetables adding volume and flavor to each serving. Lastly, the creamy pesto sauce is made with a non-traditional, high-protein ingredient. So you can have your pasta and be healthy too.

- Preheat oven to 400°F.
- To prepare the creamy pesto, in a food processor, combine; basil, garlic, two teaspoons of salt, 1/4 cup of parmesan, and cottage cheese. Blend until smooth.
- In a large sauté pan, on medium heat, add oil.
- Add chicken sausage, and continue to break up sausage as it cooks. Cook through, about 5-7 minutes.
- Remove cooked chicken sausage from the pan and set aside.
- In the same pan, add diced vegetables. Sauté on medium-high heat. Cook occasionally, stirring for 10-12 minutes or until caramelized and softened.
- Season the vegetables with Italian seasoning and one teaspoon of salt.
- Add white wine to sauteing vegetables. Use a spatula to stir and remove caramelized bits from the bottom of the pan. (Hello, flavor!)
- Next, add cooked chicken sausage, cooked pasta, and prepared creamy pesto. Stir until combined.
- Lightly spray a 9x13 pan with non-stick spray. Transfer pasta mixture to pan.
- Top the pasta with panko breadcrumbs and parmesan cheese.
- Bake uncovered for 10 minutes or until the topping is caramelized.

Note

To save some time and simplify this recipe, feel free to substitute the pesto with a 1/2 cup of store-bought pesto. Also, have some fun with the vegetables in this recipe. Use what you have on hand, what's in season, or the veggies your family loves. The white wine is optional, feel free to swap chicken stock instead.

Calories: 350 | Fat: 11 grams | Carbs: 36 grams | Protein: 29 grams | Fiber: 4 grams

Roasted vegetable & beef lasagna

Serves 14 - Serving 1/14 of prepared lasagna

10 ounces Cauliflower riced, frozen
24 ounces Marinara
12 pieces Whole wheat lasagna
   noodles, uncooked
48 ounces Cottage cheese, 4%
2 Eggs
1 ½ cups Mozzarella, shredded

Lasagna meat
1 pound Ground beef, 90/10
1 pound Chicken sausage, casing
   removed
1 teaspoon Olive oil
2 teaspoon Salt
2 tablespoon Garlic powder
2 tablespoon Onion powder
½ tablespoon Fennel seeds
1 teaspoon Ground black pepper
32 ounces Marinara, prepared

Veggies:
(or 12 cups of raw vegetables)
1 Eggplant, diced
2 Zucchini, diced
2 Bell peppers, diced
2 Onions, diced
1 tablespoon Garlic powder
1 tablespoon Dried basil
1 teaspoon Fennel seeds
1 teaspoon Red pepper flakes
1 teaspoon Lemon pepper
1 teaspoon Salt
1 teaspoon Olive oil

Lasagna is a love language,, it's the love language we all speak and respond well to. I wouldn't share a lasagna recipe with you if it weren't amazing. This lasagna is stacked with flavor (pun intended).

Veggies
- Preheat oven to 400°F.
- In a large bowl, combine diced vegetables and all of the vegetable seasonings; garlic powder, dried basil, fennel, pepper flakes, lemon pepper, salt, and olive oil
- Line a large sheet tray with parchment paper, dump coated vegetables on pan and spread out well.
- Place pan in the oven, and bake for 20-25 minutes or until the vegetables are slightly caramelized. Remove from oven, and set aside.

Lasagna meat
- In a large sauté pan, add one teaspoon of oil on medium heat.
- Then add chicken sausage removed from the casing and ground beef.
- As meat is cooking, continue to stir occasionally, breaking up the meat.
- Cook meat for 7-10 minutes. Add salt, garlic powder, onion powder, fennel, pepper, and marinara.
- Turn the heat off and set prepared meat aside.

To build the lasagna
- In a large bowl, combine eggs, cottage cheese, and mix well.
- Spray a large casserole dish with non-stick spray.
- Pour one cup of marinara into the bottom of the pan, and spread it out to all corners.
- Then top the marinara with four lasagna noodle sheets. Next, top the noodles with half of the roasted vegetables spread out well. Then half of the meat and spread out well.
- Top with half of cottage cheese mixture.
- Lay four lasagna noodle sheets, followed by the remaining vegetables spread out, meat spread evenly, and cottage cheese evenly spread.
- Lastly, top with four lasagna noodle sheets and two cups of marinara.
- Cover lasagna with aluminum foil. Then bake at 350°F for 1 hour.
- Remove from oven, and top with cheese. Bake for 15 minutes or until the cheese is melted. Allow cooling for 15-20 minutes.

Note
This recipe is massive and requires some TLC, but it is so good and worth the effort, it will feed you and your family for days! The lasagna will last up to 7 days in your fridge. To freeze any leftovers, once the lasagna is baked, cut it into 14 pieces, store cut pieces in food storage containers, and freeze for up to 6 months. When you are ready to dive in, preheat the oven to 350°F and reheat the lasagna piece for 20-30 minutes or until warmed through.

Calories: 510 | Fat: 16 grams | Carbs: 59 grams | Protein: 39 grams | Fiber: 11 grams

A twist on the classics

Some of my favorite dishes to create are recipe makeovers. Re-doing classic flavors and cooking preparations to make dishes a little healthier and easy to prepare is my love language. This chapter is reintroducing you to meals that have always been deemed as "unhealthy". By adding more vegetables, whole foods, and baking over frying these traditionally unhealthy dishes are healthy and delicious.

Crispy fish tacos

Serves 4 - Serving 2 assembled tacos

1 pound White firm fish (Mahi, grouper, snapper)
½ cup Cornmeal
½ tablespoon Chili powder
1 teaspoon Cumin
½ teaspoon Salt
¼ teaspoon Ground black pepper
1 tablespoon Avocado oil
8 Corn tortillas

Choose your favorite type of fish or use what is fresh or local. The fish is lightly breaded in a flavorful seasoned corn meal, then lightly seared for the perfect golden brown.

- Pat the fish dry with a paper towel; cut the fish crosswise into 1-inch-wide strips.
- On a plate or shallow bowl, season the cornmeal with chili powder, cumin, salt and pepper.
- Gently press the fish in the cornmeal, coating all sides.
- Preheat the sauté pan to medium-high heat.
- Add avocado oil, and allow to warm for about 10 seconds.
- Add the fish and cook, turning once, until the crust is golden brown and the fish is cooked through, 2-4 minutes per side.
- While the fish is cooking, warm the tortillas. Place tortillas on a plate, cover them with a damp paper towel, and microwave for 45 seconds.
- Once all of the fish is cooked, build your dream tacos!

Note
Have fun topping these tacos with shredded cabbage, avocado, pineapple salsa, green goddess dressing, or, as pictured street corn salad.

Calories: 300 | Fat: 6 grams | Carbs: 39 grams | Protein: 26 grams | Fiber: 5 grams

Crispy baked chicken wings

2 pounds Chicken wings, fresh
1 tablespoon Onion powder
1 tablespoon Garlic powder
½ tablespoon Smoked paprika
2 teaspoon Salt
1 teaspoon Ground black pepper
2 teaspoon Baking powder

This dish was inspired by Cindy, my mother-in-law. While we were staying with her in New Zealand, she treated us to preparing dinner night after night, and it was such a treat. Amongst many of her meals, these crispy baked chicken wings rocked my world. She shared with me the secret to the fried-like crispiness... baking powder. Baking powder allows the protein to break down more efficiently, thus crispier with more evenly browned results... amazing!

- Preheat oven to 450°F.
- Pat wings dry with a paper towel. Removing any excess moisture will help crisp up these wings.
- Toss wings with seasoning and baking powder until nicely coated.
- Place wings on a lightly greased baking rack on a sheet tray. The baking rack will elevate the wings to help move heat below them to crisp them up.
- Bake on convection (if you have that option) for 25-30 minutes or until nice and crisp! Serve with the green goddess or healthy ranch dressing.

Note

Have leftovers? Yay! Store in an airtight container in the fridge for up to 7 days. Reheat by preheating the oven to 400°F, place the wings on a lined and greased baking sheet, and bake for 10 minutes.

Calories: 330 | Fat: 23 grams | Carbs: 0 grams | Protein: 30 grams | Fiber: 0 grams

Tostadas

with smoky verde pulled pork tenderloin

GF

3 Corn tortillas

1/2 cup Refried beans, canned

2 1/2 ounces Smoky verde pulled pork
tenderloin
(see recipe page 88)

1/4 Avocado, sliced

1 cup Shredded iceberg lettuce

1 tablespoon Green goddess dressing
(see recipe page 96)

1 Roma tomato, diced

1/2 tablespoon Feta cheese, crumbled

This recipe is a healthier version of a delicious classic preparation. Baking the corn tortillas rather than frying eliminates excess calories and unsaturated fats while still delivering a satisfying, flavorful crunch. Layered with refried beans, tossed in the bright Green goddess dressing, and topped with your make-ahead verde pulled pork tenderloin, your taste buds will be so happy.

Baked crispy corn tortillas

- Preheat oven to 375°F.
- Lightly grease a sheet tray with avocado oil.
- Spread corn tortillas out onto the tray, not overlapping and not touching one another.
- Bake for 7 minutes, then flip the corn tortillas over.
- Bake for the remaining 5 minutes.
- Remove from oven and eat immediately or allow to cool. Do not stack them or put them away until they have completely cooled. (They will become stale in texture due to the steam if they are stored or stacked while warm.)

Build tostadas

- In a bowl, combine; lettuce and green goddess dressing. Toss to combine.
- Once the tortillas are baked, top each tortilla with about two tablespoons of warmed refried beans.
- Then divide the prepared pork onto each tortilla.
- Garnish each tortilla with lettuce, tomato, feta, and sliced avocado.

Nutrition Note

Refried beans are a traditional and delicious Latin American dish using pinto beans. The beans are boiled, then mashed with spices and fat to be fried in a skillet. Choose a healthier canned refried bean, check the ingredients, avoid lard and opt for plant-based oils like avocado oil. If you are in a pinch, substitute rotisserie chicken with the smoky verde pulled pork tenderloin. Garnish with limes, cilantro, jalapeno, and avocado.

Calories: 500 | Fat: 15 grams | Carbs: 60 grams | Protein: 33 grams | Fiber: 15 grams

Soul good loaded nachos

with smoky verde pulled pork tenderloin

GF

Serves 1 - Serving assembled nachos

4 Corn tortillas

½ teaspoon Salt

3 tablespoons Mozzarella, shredded

3 tablespoons Sharp cheddar,
   shredded

1/3 cup Refried beans

2 ounces Smoky verde pulled pork,
   tenderloin
   (see recipe page 88)

Garnishes

Bell peppers, diced

Red onion, diced

Iceberg lettuce, shredded

Jalapenos, sliced

Avocado, diced

Salsa

Talk about good for the soul… Nachos and healthy, all in one? Yep! Baking corn tortillas to make your chips will save on calories and excess unhealthy fats. Top these nachos with your make-ahead smoky verde pulled pork or any convenient protein, black beans, shrimp, ground beef, or grilled chicken.

- Preheat oven to 400°F.
- Cut each tortilla into six triangles, making six chips per tortilla.
- Cover a large sheet tray with parchment paper.
- Spread the tortilla triangles out onto the pan. Spread them out enough that they are not touching. Lightly spray non-stick oil over triangles and sprinkle with salt.
- Bake the tortilla triangles for 8 minutes. Remove them from the oven. Flip the chips and bake for two more minutes.
- Once the chips are crispy, push the chips together on the same sheet tray.
- Begin topping; scoop small dollops of refried beans on top of baked chips, spread the pulled pork onto the chips, and sprinkle with cheese.
- Bake for 3-4 minutes, until the cheese has melted.
- Remove from oven and top with your preferred toppings.
- Enjoy immediately.

Nutrition Note

Get wild and top this nacho stack with anything you would put on a taco. You know what to do. Trust your instinct.

Calories: 500 | Fat: 17 grams | Carbs: 53 grams | Protein: 34 grams | Fiber: 9 grams

Spicy steak sheet-tray fajitas
with roasted bell peppers & onions

Serves 6 - Serving 2 fajitas

2 Bell peppers, julienned
1 Onion, julienned
2 teaspoons Salt
1 teaspoon Red pepper flakes
1 tablespoon Oregano, dried
2 tablespoons Olive oil
12 Flour tortillas

Marinade

1 1/2 pounds Flank steak, trimmed, sliced
½ cup Lime juice, fresh
¼ cup Soy sauce
3 tablespoons Chipotle in adobo, minced
1 tablespoon Garlic, fresh, minced
1 tablespoon Cumin

Fajitas are such a simple go-to recipe. We are dialing up the flavor and the simplicity by tossing all of the ingredients on a sheet tray and knocking it all out at once. The skirt steak marinade works magic on the steak, as it tenderizes and pumps up the flavor.

- In a large bowl or plastic sealable bag, combine bell peppers, onions, salt, pepper flakes, oregano, and olive oil. Toss to combine evenly.
- In a separate large bowl or plastic sealable bag, combine steak, lime juice, soy sauce, chipotle, garlic, and cumin. Toss to combine evenly.
- Store marinated steak in the refrigerator for at least 30 minutes or up to 24 hours.
- Preheat oven to 400°F.
- Line a large sheet tray with parchment paper.
- Remove vegetables and the marinated steak from marinade and place on the same sheet tray. Evenly spread the contents.
- Bake for 12 minutes.
- Remove the sheet tray from the oven and build fajitas; 2 ounces of steak and 1/4 cup of vegetables in each tortilla.
- Garnish with; guacamole, pico de gallo, and fresh cilantro.

Note

This recipe works great with chicken too. To add a bit extra oomph... garnish your fajitas with the Green goddess dressing.

Calories: 460 | Fat: 24 grams | Carbs: 27 grams | Protein: 36 grams | Fiber: 11 grams

Healthy burritos

with chipotle cream

Serves 1 - Serving 2 assembled burritos

3 ounces Simple taco meat
  (see recipe page 89)
½ cup Refried beans, canned
2 tablespoons Bell peppers, diced
2 tablespoons Onions, diced
½ cup Iceberg lettuce, shredded
¼ Avocado, sliced
2 Flour tortillas
2 tablespoons Chipotle cream
  (see recipe page 94)

Burritos can have endless filling ingredients; salsa, romaine, avocado, etc... Batch cook the meat, sautéed peppers, and onions so you can quickly whip these up all week long. No time to whip up chipotle cream? Just add a dash of your favorite hot sauce to add some zing!

Building burritos

- Place tortillas on a microwave-safe plate, cover them with a damp paper towel, and microwave for 30 seconds. (Doing this step is essential to make the tortilla pliable and easier to shape into a burrito that can fit many goodies.)
- Start with a shmear of the chipotle cream on each tortilla. Then divide the remaining ingredients between the two tortillas.
- To wrap the burrito, fold in the opposite sides of the tortilla and roll to shape a burrito.

Note

Use the Simple taco meat recipe or Smoky verde pulled pork tenderloin recipes. If you are tight on time, substitute rotisserie chicken.

Calories: 445 | Fat: 14 grams | Carbs: 46 grams | Protein: 41 grams | Fiber: 19 grams

Buffalo chicken stuffed sweet potato

with bleu cheese crumbles

1 Sweet potato, roasted
4 ounces Chicken cooked, shredded
2 tablespoons Buffalo wing sauce
½ cup Broccoli slaw
2 tablespoons Carrots, shredded
1 tablespoon Healthy ranch dressing
   (see recipe page 96)
1 tablespoon Green onion, sliced
½ tablespoon Bleu cheese, crumbled

We are dialing up the nutrition on a delicious well-known combination, buffalo chicken. These flavors can be served in a healthy fashion by using baked chicken, a homemade ranch dressing, and bulking up the veggies. The sweet potato is the perfect vehicle for this combo; the sweetness plays well with the spicy buffalo sauce.

- In a mixing bowl, combine warmed cooked chicken and buffalo sauce.
- In a separate mixing bowl, combine broccoli slaw, carrots, and ranch dressing.
- Split open warmed, roasted sweet potato, top with chicken, then broccoli slaw, green onions, and bleu cheese.

Note

Bake, grill, or slow cook the chicken, or make your life easier, and use a rotisserie chicken. Additionally, I recommend roasting multiple sweet potatoes at a time. Doing so will allow you to remake this dish throughout the week or use the sweet potato for other meals.

Calories: 385 | Fat: 10 grams | Carbs: 33 grams | Protein: 40 grams | Fiber: 6 grams

BBQ chicken pizza

with red onion, bell peppers, & pineapple

Serves 1 - Serving 1 assembled pizza

1 Pita bread
2 ½ ounces Chicken, cooked
5 tablespoons BBQ sauce, divided
1/8 teaspoon Red pepper flakes
½ teaspoon Chili powder
2 tablespoons Red onion, diced
3 tablespoons Bell pepper, diced
2 tablespoons Pineapple, diced
3 tablespoons Mozzarella, shredded
3 tablespoons Cheddar, shredded

I love pizza! Pizza loves us too. It's for everyone! Even the pickiest eaters love to nosh on it. These individual pizzas allow everyone to pick and choose what they'd like to toss on their crust.

- Preheat the oven to 425°F.
- Place the pita on a lightly greased sheet tray. Spread two tablespoons of BBQ sauce onto the pita.
- In a separate bowl, combine chicken, three tablespoons of BBQ sauce, chili powder, and crushed red pepper flakes.
- Top the pita with the seasoned chicken.
- Top the seasoned chicken with onions, bell peppers, pineapple, and cheese.
- Bake for 15 minutes or until the crust is crispy, the cheese is melted, and golden brown.

Note

Making pizza is a great way to use leftover vegetable and protein prep. Weekly pizza nights keep the family happy and the fridge cleaned out.

Calories: 490 | Fat: 16 grams | Carbs: 49 grams | Protein: 39 grams | Fiber: 4 grams

Zucchini & herb turkey burgers

2 pounds Ground turkey breast
2 small Zucchini, shredded (~2 cups)
1 cup Mozzarella, shredded
1/4 cup Garlic, minced
1/2 cup Onion, yellow, minced
1 tablespoon Salt
2 teaspoons Black pepper
1 bunch Parsley, minced

Burger topping ideas
Crumbled goat cheese
Sliced pickels
Chipotle cream
  (see recipe page 94)
Arugula
Sliced tomato
Sliced onion

Burgers can be made healthier and still taste incredible! This burger calls for ground turkey breast; it's lean and high in protein. The game changer is combining the turkey with fresh herbs, garlic, onion, and shredded zucchini to add layers of flavor. Adding herbs and veggies creates a perfectly moist and tender burger patty.

- In a large bowl, combine all ingredients: ground turkey, zucchini, mozzarella, garlic, onion, salt, pepper, and parsley.
- Blend well.
- Portion out the meat mixture into ~4-ounce patties.
- Preheat the grill and lightly grease the grill grates.
- Place the burgers on the grill and cook for 4-5 minutes or until the turkey burger easily flips. (If the burger is sticking, it needs more time to cook, don't flip it.)
- Flip and cook for 4-5 more minutes or until the internal temperature reaches 165°F.
- Serve with your favorite toppings and burger bun.

Nutrition Note

Think of fresh herbs as mini vegetables! Fresh herbs are nutrient and flavor dense. To pump up the flavor and nutrition of your meals, include fresh herbs in recipes when you can. To get ahead, make a large batch of the turkey burgers, shape the patties, spread them on a parchment-lined sheet tray, and freeze them for 4-6 hours. Once frozen, remove the patties and place in storage containers and keep in the freezer for pre-made frozen turkey burgers. Throw them straight on the grill and cook through when it's time to dig in.

Calories: 200 | Fat: 5 grams | Carbs: 7 grams | Protein: 31 grams | Fiber: 2 grams

Simple seafood

Weeknights can be wild. Whether you are doing the carpool shuffle, coming home from a long workday, or just desire a simple, quick meal, these recipes are for you. Healthy food doesn't require an entire day of meal prep nor hours of chopping vegetables. Toss these meals together for a simple and satisfying meal.

Mediterranean salmon en papillote

with artichokes, tomatoes, bell peppers, & olives

Serves 2 - Serving 1 assembled pouch

2 (4-ounce filets) Salmon filets

2 teaspoons Italian seasoning

1/4 teaspoon Red pepper flakes

½ teaspoon Salt

¼ teaspoon Ground black pepper

1 Lemon, sliced

4 cloves Garlic, sliced

½ cup Artichokes, canned, quartered

½ cup Bell pepper, diced

2 tablespoons Kalamata olives, quartered

2 tablespoons Red onion, diced

½ cup Cherry tomatoes, halved

En papillote is French for "in paper", it is a method of cooking in which food is wrapped or put into a folded pouch and baked. Wrapping and baking the pouch creates a steaming method, creating a marriage of flavors. En papillote sounds far fancier than paper, so stick with it.

- Preheat oven to 425°F.
- In a small bowl, combine Italian seasoning, red pepper flakes, salt, and ground black pepper.
- Fold two pieces of parchment paper in half and center each filet on one side of each paper. Squeeze fresh lemon juice on each salmon filet and sprinkle each filet with seasoning mix.
- Divide the vegetables in half and arrange the garlic, artichokes, olives, onions, bell peppers, and tomatoes over and around the two filets.
- Fold the parchment paper over the fish. Fold the edges of the paper over several times, inch by inch, all around the open edges to seal the fish into a parchment paper envelope. (Do not tape the parchment paper closed.)
- Place the sealed envelopes onto a baking sheet.
- Bake in the preheated oven until the fish is opaque, about 12 minutes. To serve, place the baked envelope onto a plate, and cut open the paper to release the aroma.
- Serve with fresh arugula and roasted potatoes.

Note

This preparation is very diverse; feel free to swap out different seafood in this dish, mahi mahi, grouper, or shrimp would be great. The Mediterranean salmon en papillote is packed with flavor, loaded with nutrition, and there are minimal dirty dishes.

Calories: 335 calories | Fat: 12 grams | Carbs: 25 grams | Protein: 34 grams | Fiber: 11 grams

Miso peanut shrimp

1 teaspoon Sesame oil
2 pounds Shrimp, peeled and deveined
1 cup Miso peanut sauce
  (see recipe page 94)
1 teaspoon Red pepper flakes
1 tablespoon Cornstarch
2 tablespoons Water, cold

There are many reasons why I adore shrimp. First, it's a great protein, and second, it cooks quickly. Serve this shrimp with coconut fried rice for a swoon-worthy meal in minutes.

- In a large sauté pan, on medium heat, add sesame oil.
- Meanwhile, lay thawed shrimp on a paper towel lined sheet tray. Pat shrimp with paper towels to absorb extra moisture. (Eliminating excess water ensures a crispy sear.)
- Add shrimp to the warmed pan, and allow to sear for 2-3 minutes.
- Combine cornstarch and cold water. Set aside.
- Add miso peanut sauce and red pepper flakes. Stir.
- Slowly add cornstarch and water mixture while stirring. Add until the sauce has reached your desired thickness.
- Remove from heat and enjoy.

Note

Not a spicy fan? No problem, skip the added crushed red pepper flakes or only add a pinch.

Calories: 275 | Fat: 9 grams | Carbs: 11 grams | Protein: 35 grams | Fiber: 2 grams

Chili-rubbed salmon
with pineapple salsa

1 teaspoon Avocado oil
4 Salmon filets, 5 ounces each
1 tablespoon Chili powder
1 teaspoon Garlic powder
1 teaspoon Cumin
1/2 teaspoon Salt
1/8 teaspoon Ground black pepper
1 cup Pineapple salsa
  (see recipe page 95)

Dial up the flavor profile of salmon with a light dusting of savory and smoky seasonings. Utilizing dry spices is a simple way to add flavor.

- Preheat the grill to medium-high heat.
- In a small bowl, combine seasoning, chili powder, garlic powder, cumin, salt, and pepper. Season salmon liberally on both sides.
- Once the grill is preheated (~400°F-450°F), lightly grease the grill grates with oil. Then, place seasoned salmon and sear on one side for 4-6 minutes, flip, and repeat. Continue to grill the salmon until it easily comes off the grill grates and the internal temperature reaches ~140-145°F
- Remove the perfectly cooked salmon from the grill and top with 1/4 cup of prepared pineapple salsa.

Note

The Chili-rubbed salmon is the perfect dish to add to your spring and summer meal rotation. Mix it up using different seafood; scallops, grouper, mahi mahi, or tuna. For a balanced dish, serve this salmon with steamed coconut rice and roasted green beans.

Calories: 250 | Fat: 8 grams | Carbs: 7 grams | Protein: 37 grams| Fiber: 1 gram

Working smarter

Simplify your life by making larger batches of proteins, and cross-utilizing them throughout the week. Aim to make one large batch of protein weekly and use it to make: wraps, tacos, pizzas, bowls, or salads. Having prepared proteins on hand makes whipping up a meal a breeze.

Lemon dijon marinated chicken

Serves 4 - Serving 4 ounces

2 pounds Chicken breast
1/4 cup Dijon mustard
1/4 cup Soy sauce, low sodium
1 tablespoon Italian seasoning
1 tablespoon Onion powder
1 tablespoon Garlic powder
1 each Lemon, juiced (~1/4 cup)

An easy chicken that everyone will love, this goes with almost everything. Our secret is using soy sauce in the marinade. Soy sauce envelops the chicken with an umami flavor. Plus, lemon juice helps tenderize the chicken.

- Trim chicken breast, removing excess fat and tendons. Cut chicken breast into long thick strips.
- Place chicken breast in a large plastic storage bag or bowl.
- Add all ingredients to the chicken.
- Massage the marinade into the chicken breast.
- Marinate for at least 1 hour or up to 2 days.
- Grill, bake, or sear chicken breast.
- To grill, preheat the grill to medium heat. Allow the grill to warm for up to 10 minutes.
- Lightly grease grill grates.
- Using tongs, remove chicken from the bag, shake off excess marinade, and place on preheated grill.
- Grill for 6-9 minutes, flip chicken breast and allow to cook for another 6-9 minutes. Cook chicken until internal temperature reaches 160°F-165°F.

Note

Marinate a large batch, grill, cool, and refrigerate for up to 7 days to use throughout the entire week. If you don't get through everything you have prepped, freeze the grilled chicken for up to 6 months. To thaw, place in the fridge overnight, reheat, and enjoy.

Calories: 160 | Fat: 3 grams | Carbs: 0 grams | Protein: 30 grams | Fiber: 0 grams

Smoky verde pulled pork tenderloin

2 pounds Pork tenderloin
2 teaspoons Salt
1 cup Salsa verde
1 tablespoon Smoked paprika
1/4 teaspoon Red pepper flakes
1/2 tablespoon Cumin

Pork tenderloin is a lean and tender cut of meat. We are jazzing it up with prepared salsa and seasonings.

Instant pot/pressure cooker method

- Set your instant pot on sauté. Allow warming for 2-3 minutes.
- Lightly spray the bottom of the pan with non-stick spray.
- Trim pork tenderloin by removing excess fat and tendons.
- Cut the pork tenderloin into 2-3-inch large chunks.
- Place pork tenderloin into the preheated instant pot. Allow to sauté without moving pork for about 3 minutes. Then stir and allow to sauté for 3-4 more minutes.
- Next, add salt, salsa, smoked paprika, red pepper flakes, and cumin.
- Place the lid on the instant pot and close the "chimney."
- Switch the cooking method to pressure cook.
- Pressure cook on high for 30 minutes.
- Once the 30 minutes is up, release the pressure, until it drops completely.
- Use forks or tongs to easily shred the pork. It will be incredibly tender, and minimal effort will be needed.

Slow cooker method

- Line your slow cooker with a slow cooker liner. (This makes clean-up a breeze!)
- Trim pork tenderloin by removing excess fat and tendons.
- Cut the pork tenderloin into 2-3-inch large chunks.
- Next, add all ingredients. And stir.
- Place lid on the slow cooker.
- Cook on high for 6-8 hours. The pork tenderloin will be incredibly tender, use a fork to easily shred the meat.

Note

Use either the slow-cooker or instant-pot method, whichever you prefer. Either way, it will be tasty and easy. Store in the fridge for up to 7 days or freeze for 6 months.

Calories: 180 | Fat: 5 grams | Carbs: 1 gram | Protein: 30 grams | Fiber: 0 grams

Simple taco meat

2 pounds Ground turkey breast
¼ teaspoon Avocado oil
½ cup Salsa verde
1 tablespoon Cumin
1 tablespoon Oregano, dried
2 tablespoons Chili powder
1 teaspoon Salt
½ teaspoon Red pepper flakes

No need to purchase the prepackaged seasoning! This recipe is easy and so flavorful. It's a versatile recipe; it's great for tacos, taco salads, nachos, burritos, or enchiladas.

- Place a large sauté pan over medium heat. Warm for about 10 seconds.
- Add oil.
- Add ground turkey breast.
- Cook turkey breast stirring occasionally, use a spatula to break it into small pieces while cooking.
- Once the turkey is about 90% cooked, add all seasonings; salsa, cumin, oregano, chili powder, salt, and red pepper flakes.
- Continue to cook on medium-low heat until turkey is cooked through, about 3-4 more minutes.

Note

Feel free to swap out different proteins in place of the ground turkey. To mix it up try, 1 pound of ground turkey and 1 pound of lean ground beef or all ground beef. Using ground turkey is a high protein source and low in fat content. Make a large batch and freeze it for up to 6 months.

Calories: 125 | Fat: 2 grams | Carbs: 1 gram | Protein: 26 grams| Fiber: 0 grams

elevate your dish

Sauces and dressings are where the flavor is! These recipes can be made in large batches to be stored in your fridge or freezer for months. Mix and match these recipes with different dishes; they are packed with flavor and will dial up any meal.

Sauces & Dressings

Feeling saucy

Zesty strawberry syrup

Chipotle cream

Chipotle enchilada sauce

Miso peanut sauce

Pineapple salsa

Chimichurri sauce

Dress it up

Green goddess dressing

Healthy ranch dressing

Honey dijon vinaigrette

Basil pesto vinaigrette

Jalapeno cilantro dressing

 Vegetarian   Vegan   Gluten Free   Dairy Free

Feeling saucy

Sauces can quickly elevate a meal. Using whole foods as the base creates a nutrient-dense and flavorful sauce. Get saucy!

Zesty strawberry syrup

Serves 6 - Serving 1/4 cup

10 ounces Strawberries, frozen, sliced
1 teaspoon Orange zest
1/4 cup Maple syrup
1 tablespoon Cornstarch
1 tablespoon Water, cold

Serve this bright zesty sauce on top of pancakes, oatmeal, or French toast. It's a great alternative to that heavy drizzle of maple syrup. The strawberries are packed with fiber, vitamin C, and manganese.

- In a medium saucepot, add strawberries and cook on low-medium heat.
- As the strawberries thaw and release their juices, continue to stir.
- Once the strawberries have thawed, add orange zest, and maple syrup.
- Then combine corn starch and water, to create a slurry.
- While stirring the strawberry mixture, slowly pour in the cornstarch slurry.
- The sauce will thicken immediately. Cook for and additional minute.
- Remove from heat, and serve warm.

Calories: 50 | Fat: 0 grams | Carbs: 13 grams | Protein: 0 grams | Fiber: 1 gram

Chipotle cream

16 ounces Cottage cheese, 4%
5 Chipotle peppers in adobo sauce
3 tablespoons Adobo sauce
1 tablespoon Garlic powder
1 tablespoon Smoked paprika
½ teaspoon Salt

I was inspired to create this recipe after dining at a local dive bar. I submerged my entire meal in their chipotle ranch dip. Since then, I have been on a mission to recreate that goodness. This chipotle cream lives up to the hype. Schmear on burgers, wraps, and tacos.

- Combine all ingredients in food processor and blend until smooth.

Calories: 30 | Fat: 1 gram | Carbs: 1 gram | Protein: 4 grams | Fiber: 0 grams

Chipotle enchilada sauce

Makes 2 1/2 cups - Serving 1/2 cup

3-4 each Chipotle peppers, in adobo
3 each Garlic cloves
2 1/2 tablespoons Chili powder
2 teaspoons Cumin
2 teaspoons Oregano, dried
1 teaspoon Salt
29 ounces Tomato sauce, canned

This sauce is upping the ante for all things enchilada. It takes a little extra effort to make it homemade, yet the flavor is well worth it.

- In a food processor add all ingredients.
- Blend until smooth.

Note
Chipotle peppers in adobo add great depth of flavor and smokiness. However, they are spicy! Add 3, taste it, and add more if you like some heat.

Calories: 45 | Fat: 1 gram | Carbs: 10 grams | Protein: 2 grams | Fiber: 3 grams

Miso peanut sauce

Serves 18- Serving 2 tablespoons

1/4 cup Powdered peanut butter
1/2 cup Peanut butter, natural
1/4 cup Ginger, fresh, minced
2 tablespoons Miso paste, yellow
1/4 teaspoon Red pepper flakes
1 /2 cup Water
1/4 cup Soy sauce, low sodium
2 tablespoons Agave

This tasty sauce goes on juuuust about everything.

- Combine all ingredients in a blender, blend until smooth.

Calories: 60 | Fat: 4 grams | Carbs: 6 grams | Protein: 3 grams | Fiber: 1 gram

Pineapple salsa

Serves 4 - Serving 1/4 cup

1 cup Pineapple, small diced
1/4 cup Red bell pepper, small diced
1/4 cup Red onion, small diced
2 tablespoons Cilantro, minced
1 Lime, juiced
½ teaspoon Salt
¼ teaspoon Ground black pepper

This pineapple salsa has a delicious combination of sweet and spicy. It can be served on grilled fish, tacos, steak, or as an appetizer with chips.

- Combine all prepped ingredients in a bowl.
- Serve cold.
- Store in refrigerator for up to 5 days.

Calories: 25 | Fat: 0 grams | Carbs: 6 grams | Protein: 0 grams | Fiber: 1 gram

Chimichurri sauce

Serves 24 - Serving 1 tablespoon

1 1/2 cups Parsley, packed
1/2 cup Cilantro, packed
1/4 cup Oregano, packed
1/4 Red onion
3 Garlic cloves
3 tablespoons Red wine vinegar
2 tablespoons Lemon juice, fresh
1 teaspoon Salt
1/4 teaspoon Red pepper flakes
3/4 cup Olive oil

Chimichurri is incredibly vibrant, it's jam-packed with fresh herbs and flavor.

- Add red onion, garlic, red wine vinegar, lemon juice, and salt to a food processor.
- Pulse, stopping and scraping down sides occasionally until finely minced.
- Add in parsley, cilantro, oregano, and red pepper flakes, then pour in olive oil while pulsing several times until herb leaves are finely minced.

Nutrition Note
Don't discount the power of fresh herbs, think of fresh herbs as mini leafy greens. For example, parsley, oregano, and cilantro are excellent sources of micronutrients, including; Vitamins A, K, and C. Drizzle this nutrient and flavor packed sauce on steak, fish, rice dishes, tacos, and so much more.

Calories: 70 | Fat: 7 grams | Carbs: 1 gram | Protein: 0 grams | Fiber: 0 grams

Dress it up

We all know the true star of a salad is the dressing. These dressings are loaded with flavor to make your salad life crave-able!

Green goddess dressing

Serves 16 - Serving 2 tablespoons

1 cup Cilantro leaves, fresh
1 cup Basil leaves, fresh,
1/4 cup Tarragon leaves, fresh
3 tablespoons Dijon mustard
1 tablespoon Honey
1/2 cup Water
1 cup Cottage cheese, 4%
2 tablespoons Garlic, fresh
1/2 teaspoon Salt
1/4 teaspoon Black pepper

A dressing made of heaps of greens, to then put on more heaps of greens! Nutrition and flavor at its finest. This dressing is loaded with flavor, and it's good on just about everything. Make this entire batch to store in your fridge to toss it on all the things.

- In a food processor combine all ingredients.
- Blend until smooth.

Calories: 30 | Fat: 1 gram | Carbs: 3 grams | Protein: 2 grams | Fiber: 0 grams

Healthy ranch dressing

Serves 16 - Serving 2 tablespoons

16 ounces Cottage cheese, 4%
1 tablespoon Garlic powder
1 tablespoon Onion powder
1 tablespoon Apple cider vinegar
1/4 cup Water
2 teaspoons Honey
2 teaspoons Salt
1 teaspoon Ground black pepper
1/4 cup Parsley, fresh, minced

A much healthier take on a traditional and delicious dressing.

- In a food processor, combine all ingredients except the parsley.
- Once the ingredients are combined, fold in the fresh parsley.

Calories: 30 | Fat: 1 gram | Carbs: 2 grams | Protein: 3 grams | Fiber: 0 grams

Honey dijon vinaigrette

1 cup White balsamic vinegar
1 cup Dijon mustard
¼ cup Honey
¼ cup Olive oil

An adult spin on the classic honey mustard dressing. The dijon mustard and white balsamic elevate this vinaigrette.

- Place all ingredients in a blender and blend until smooth.

Calories: 35 | Fat: 0 grams | Carbs: 6 grams | Protein: 0 grams | Fiber: 0 grams

Basil pesto vinaigrette

Serves 16 - Serving 1 tablespoon

1 cup/3 ounces Basil, fresh, packed
½ cup White balsamic vinegar
1 tablespoon Dijon mustard
1 tablespoon Agave
1/4 cup Olive oil

If you love basil, you will fall madly in love with this vinaigrette. It's fresh, bright, and pairs well with so many dishes.

- In a food processor combine all ingredients except the parsley.
- Once the ingredients are combined, fold in fresh parsley.

Calories: 35 | Fat: 3 grams | Carbs: 2 grams | Protein: 0 grams | Fiber: 0 grams

Jalepeno cilantro dressing

Serves 16 - Serving 1 tablespoon

2 cups Cottage cheese, 4%
2 Jalapeno peppers
1/4 cup Verde salsa
1 tablespoon Honey
1 cup Cilantro, stems removed
1 tablespoon Garlic powder
2 teaspoons Salt

This dressing is perfection. It's delicately spicy with a touch of sweetness. It's great for taco salads, grilled seafood, wraps, or chicken salads.

- Remove the seeds from one jalapeno and chop, roughly chop the other.
- In a food processor combine all ingredients, blend until smooth.

Calories: 50 | Fat: 2 grams | Carbs: 4 grams | Protein: 4 grams | Fiber: 0 grams

on the side

When planning meals, it's common to plan the protein first, and the side dishes get the last-minute thought. Say bye-bye to that way of life! Side dishes can add nutrition, balance, and satiety to your meals. These recipes are simple, packed with nutrition, and delicious.

Side dishes

Healthy carbohydrates
Coconut fried rice
Steamed coconut rice
Patatas bravas
Parmesan truffle hassleback potatoes

Flavor-forward veggies
Roasted spiced carrots
Roasted green beans
Coconut thai braised brussel sprouts
Roasted vegetables

V Vegetarian   VE Vegan   GF Gluten Free   DF Dairy Free

Healthy carbohydrates

Carbohydrates are good for the soul and good for the body.
The recipes in this section will add balance, variety, nutrition, and goodness to your plate.

Coconut fried rice

Serves 9 - Serving 1 cup

3 cups Steamed coconut rice
  (see recipe page 104)
1 tablespoon Sesame oil
2 Eggs, whisked
1 cup Cauliflower, raw, "riced"/minced
1 Bell pepper, diced
1 cup Carrot, small diced
1/2 cup Green peas
1 cup Pineapple, diced
1/2 cup Green onion, sliced
1/4 cup Soy sauce, low sodium

This delicious coconut fried rice is layered with flavors that will leave your taste buds wanting more.

- In a large sauté pan, add 1/2 of sesame oil on medium-high heat. Add cauliflower, bell pepper, and carrots. Sauté for 3-5 minutes, stirring occasionally.
- In a separate small sauté pan, heat the pan to medium heat. Spray with non-stick spray, and add eggs. Scramble eggs. Set aside.
- Remove vegetables from the pan, and set aside. Add remaining oil, and allow to warm.
- Add prepared coconut rice. Sauté for 4-5 minutes, stirring occasionally, and allow the rice to toast and slightly caramelize. Then add cooked cauliflower mixture, eggs, green peas, pineapple, green onion, and soy sauce.
- Combine, and allow to cook for 4-5 minutes more until green peas and pineapple have warmed through.

Nutrition Note
We are adding a lot of flavor and nutrients to this recipe with additional veggies. The cauliflower will blend in with the rice, adding volume to each portion. Serve this rice with the miso peanut shrimp, seafood, or sauteed chicken for a balanced and mouthwatering meal.

Calories: 160 | Fat: 5 grams | Carbs: 25 grams | Protein: 5 grams | Fiber: 3 grams

Steamed coconut rice

1/2 tablespoon Coconut oil
2 cups Jasmin rice
2 cups Coconut milk, full fat
2 cups Water
2 tablespoons Coconut extract
2 teaspoons Salt
1/2 teaspoon Ground black pepper

A delicate coconut flavor and a hint of sweetness will make this rice one of your go-to side dishes!

- In a medium saucepot on high heat, add coconut oil. Add rice and toast. About 3-4 minutes, stirring occasionally.
- Then add coconut milk, water, extract, salt, and pepper. Turn the heat to high and allow the mixture to boil.
- Once the mixture reaches a boil, turn the heat down to low and put a lid on top of the pot.
- The rice will cook within 17-20 minutes or until all of the liquid has been absorbed, and the rice is al dente.

Note

Prepare a large batch of the coconut rice, cool it in the fridge, divide it among storage containers and freeze what you won't use within seven days. To thaw, remove coconut rice from the freezer and place it in the fridge overnight.

Calories: 145 | Fat: 3 grams | Carbs: 26 grams | Protein: 2 grams | Fiber: 2 grams

Patatas bravas

4 medium Potatoes, skin-on, diced
1/2 tablespoon Olive oil
3 tablespoons Mayonnaise
1 tablespoon White vinegar
½ teaspoon Salt
¼ teaspoon Red pepper flakes
1 tablespoon Chili powder
½ tablespoon Garlic powder
1 teaspoon Smoked paprika
1 teaspoon Cumin

Patatas bravas meaning "spicy potatoes," is a traditional Spanish tapa. Traditionally, the potato cubes are fried and tossed in a spicy sauce. I love this preparation; however, I wanted to make it healthier. So, by baking the potatoes, we reduce excess saturated fats and calories but yield a crispy potato, then we toss it with a flavorful combination of spices. The mayonnaise adds thickness to the sauce, and the vinegar adds a welcomed tang.

- Preheat oven to 400°F.
- In a large bowl, combine potatoes and olive oil.
- Spread potatoes onto a parchment-lined sheet tray.
- Once the potatoes are golden brown and crispy, remove them from the oven. (About 25-30 minutes)
- Meanwhile, combine mayonnaise, vinegar, salt, pepper flakes, chili powder, garlic powder, smoked paprika, and cumin in a bowl.
- Combine roasted potatoes with spice mixture, and toss until evenly coated. Serve warm.

Note

Patatas bravas are incredible as a side dish. They are likely the star of the plate, keep your protein simple, and let the potatoes shine. Also, don't limit this dish to dinner; these leftovers make an incredible morning hash.

Calories: 120 calories | Fat: 6 grams | Carbs: 16 grams | Protein: 2 grams | Fiber: 3 grams

Parmesan truffle hasselback potatoes

Serves 5 - Serving 1 potato

5 each Yukon Gold potatoes
2 tablespoons Butter, melted, divided
1 teaspoon Salt
1/2 teaspoon Ground black pepper
1/2 tablespoon Garlic powder
1/2 tablespoon Onion powder
3 tablespoons Parmesan, shredded
2 tablespoons Truffle oil

The name hasselback comes from a restaurant in Stockholm, Sweden, named Hasselbacken, where the recipe was first introduced in the 1940s. The thin, seasoned layers of the potato crisp up nicely while the base remains perfectly tender. This preparation looks fancy and tastes incredible, yet it is a simple way to elevate your side dish.

- Preheat the oven to 425°F.
- To cut the potatoes, use a large kitchen spoon to aid in this process; place the potato in the spoon and slice; the spoon will stop the knife from cutting through the potato. Hold the end of one potato. Use a sharp knife to cut across the potato to create 1/16-inch to 1/8-inch sections. Do not cut through the potato; cut two-thirds down, leaving at least a 1/2-inch solid base.
- Repeat with the remaining potatoes.
- Combine; melted butter, salt, pepper, onion powder, and garlic powder.
- Place potatoes in a large mixing bowl, pour half of the butter on the potatoes, and toss to combine.
- Place the potatoes on the baking sheet and set them cut side up. Roast in the oven for 30-40 minutes.
- Use a pastry brush to brush the remaining butter over each potato's top and between the folds. Top potatoes with parmesan cheese.
- Roast in the oven for another 10 minutes until the largest potato is fork tender.

Nutrition Note

Did you know potatoes contain more potassium than bananas? One potato contains about 600 milligrams of potassium, vitamin C, magnesium, and fiber.

Calories: 210 | Fat: 11 grams | Carbs: 26 grams | Protein: 4 grams | Fiber: 2 grams

Flavor-forward veggies

Vegetables don't have to be the weak link on our plates. The trick is to give the vegetables a little more attention. A little extra seasoning and proper cooking techniques go a long way in flavor.

Roasted spiced carrots

Serves 4 - Serving 1 cup

8 ounces Carrots
1 teaspoon Olive oil
1 teaspoon Garlic powder
1 teaspoon Onion powder
1 teaspoon Five spice
½ teaspoon Salt
½ teaspoon Ground black pepper

Roasting carrots brings out the subtle sweetness, and pairing that sweetness with spice, is a fun combination. Five spice is a spice mixture commonly used in Hawaiian and Vietnamese cuisine. While there are many variants, the common spices in the mix include star anise, cloves, cinnamon, fennel, and pepper.

- Preheat oven to 425°F.
- Combine all ingredients in a large bowl.
- Lightly spray a sheet tray or line it with parchment paper.
- Spread spiced carrots evenly on a sheet tray.
- Roast for 12-15 minutes, or until carrots are slightly caramelized and fork tender.

Note

Five-spice mixtures can typically be found at your local store in the spice aisle.

Calories: 35 | Fat: 1 gram | Carbs: 5 grams | Protein: 0 grams | Fiber: 2 grams

Roasted green beans

Serves 3 - Serving 1 cup

6 cups Green beans
1 tablespoon Olive oil
¼ teaspoon Salt
¼ teaspoon Ground black pepper

Who doesn't love food you can eat with your fingers? They aren't quite French fries, but they are salty, crunchy, and delicious!

- Preheat oven to 400°F.
- In a medium-sized bowl, add oil, salt, and pepper.
- Then toss green beans until they are evenly coated with oil and spices.
- Place green beans on a lightly greased baking sheet.
- Roast in the oven for about 20-30 minutes or until caramelized.

Note

Use this same cooking method with other vegetables to crisp them up and make them enjoyable to eat. Substitute broccoli, kale, brussel sprouts, cauliflower, or peppers.

Calories: 100 | Fat: 5 grams | Carbs: 14 grams | Protein: 4 grams | Fiber: 5 grams

Coconut thai braised brussel sprouts

Serves 6 - Serving 3/4 cup

1 teaspoon Coconut oil
2 tablespoons Peanut butter, natural
1 Lime, juiced
16 ounces Brussel sprouts, fresh, quartered
1/2 cup Coconut milk
½ teaspoon Red pepper flakes
1 teaspoon Salt
1/2 tablespoon Curry powder
1 tablespoon Cilantro chopped

This recipe gives brussel sprouts, the underestimated cruciferous vegetable, the glow-up of the year. Sweet, creamy coconut milk paired with spiced curry and crushed red pepper flakes puts these veggies on the map!

- Preheat a large sauté pan on medium-high heat.
- Add coconut oil.
- Add quartered brussels. Sauté for 4-5 minutes, allowing the brussels to caramelize and sear.
- In a small bowl, combine, coconut milk, peanut butter, lime juice, pepper flakes, salt, and curry powder.
- Adjust the heat to low.
- Add coconut mixture to brussel sprouts, and cover. Simmer for 6-9 minutes.
- Garnish with fresh cilantro.

Note

When sautéing the brussel sprouts, allow for a nice sear to occur. Avoid over-stirring; allow the brussels to sear for 3-5 minutes. The caramelization does wonders for these mini cabbages.

Calories: 110 | Fat: 8 grams | Carbs: 9 grams | Protein: 4 grams| Fiber: 3 grams

Roasted vegetables

Serves 6 - Serving 1/2 cup

2 Zucchini
1 Yellow squash
1 Onion, red
1 tablespoon Olive oil
1 teaspoon Salt
½ teaspoon Ground black pepper
1 tablespoon Garlic powder

This preparation is simple yet very important. Roasted vegetables should be crisp on the outside yet tender, not mushy in the center. Roasted vegetables are a great addition to what you are already preparing. Toss roasted vegetables into risotto, pastas, salads, wraps, and pizza.

- Preheat oven to 400°F.
- Cut vegetables into medium size chunks about the size of a quarter (they will shrink as they cook).
- In a medium-sized bowl, add oil, salt, pepper, and garlic powder. Toss chopped vegetables until they are evenly coated with oil and spices.
- Place vegetables on a lightly greased baking sheet. Roast in the oven for about 30-40 minutes, or until caramelized. Remove from oven, and allow to cool.

Note

Make sure the vegetables are spread out nicely on the pan, allowing the steam to evaporate rather than steaming the vegetables next to it. Also, if you have the convection setting on your oven, use it.

Calories: 60 | Fat: 3 grams | Carbs: 9 grams | Fiber: 2 grams | Protein: 2 grams

sweet treats

My name is Karla, and I love sweets. Who's with me?

My Dad said it best, "Everything in moderation... Including moderation..." (wink, wink) A healthy lifestyle doesn't mean, zero treats.

All of these dessert recipes are created to be crave-able, crowd-pleasing, and 250 calories or less. Dig in.

Desserts

Chocolate indulgence
- German chocolate whoopie pies
- Chocolate chip cookies
- Pumpkin spice chocolate chip muffins
- Fudge brownies
- Chocolate berry quesadilla
- Red velvet cookie bars
- Healthy chocolate pretzel cups

Seasonally sweet
- Oat crumble baked peaches
- Squeeze the day lemon bar
- Raspberry & chocolate clafoutis
- Berry bread pudding

Ⓥ Vegetarian Ⓥ Ⓔ Vegan Ⓖ Ⓕ Gluten Free Ⓓ Ⓕ Dairy Free

Chocolate indulgence

Wellness and eating healthy are all about balance.
These recipes are thoughtfully prepared to feed your soul and satisfy your chocolate cravings.

German chocolate whoopie pies

Serves 16 - Serving 1 assembled whoopie pie

2 1/2 scoops Chocolate protein powder (75 grams)
1 cup Flour, whole wheat
1 tablespoon Baking powder
1/2 teaspoon Salt
1/2 cup Cocoa powder
1/3 cup Greek yogurt
1 Egg
1/2 cup Brown sugar
1 teaspoon Vanilla extract
3/4 cup Water

Filling:
1 1/2 cups Almond milk, unsweetened vanilla
1 cup Pecans, chopped
1 cup Coconut, shredded, unsweetened
1/4 cup Honey
1 tablespoon Vanilla extract
1/8 teaspoon Salt
3 tablespoons Cornstarch
4 tablespoon Cold water

This recipe makes me want to jump and holler, "whoopie!". It's such a fun dessert. This heaven-sent filling will make you want to jump and celebrate too!

- Preheat oven to 375°F.
- Combine protein powder, flour, baking powder, salt, and cocoa powder in a medium-large mixing bowl.
- In a separate bowl, combine wet ingredients: yogurt, egg, sugar, vanilla, and water.
- Combine the dry ingredients with the wet; mixing until just combined.
- Line a baking sheet with parchment paper, scoop one tablespoon of batter onto the pan, placing 1 inch apart from the next.
- Bake for 7-9 minutes. Remove from oven and allow to cool.

Filling
- In a medium saucepan, add almond milk, vanilla, honey, and salt. Warm on medium-low.
- Allow mixture to warm to a simmer (small bubbles). Add coconut and pecans.
- In a separate small bowl, combine cornstarch and water. Mix well.
- Slowly pour the cornstarch mixture into the simmering pecan and coconut mixture. Stir while pouring in cornstarch.
- The mixture should thicken within seconds. Turn the heat off and allow the mixture to cool.
- Scoop two tablespoons of mixture onto one cookie, and sandwich it with another cookie.
- Repeat until all whoopie pies are partnered up.

Nutrition Note
To make this tasty treat a more health conscience recipe, we have added chocolate protein powder to increase the protein and yogurt in place of butter. One sandwich is the perfect satisfying portion.

Calories: 150 | Fat: 5 grams | Carbs: 21 grams | Protein: 6 grams | Fiber: 3 grams

Chocolate chip cookies

1/2 cup Brown sugar, packed

1 Egg

4 tablespoons Butter, unsalted, softened

1/2 tablespoon Vanilla extract

1 1/2 cups Almond flour

½ cup Old fashion oats

1/4 teaspoon Salt

1/2 teaspoon Baking soda

1/2 cup Milk chocolate chips

Every home should have a go-to, no-fuss chocolate chip cookie recipe. That was the goal when I created this recipe. These cookies are chewy, soft, and irresistible, yet, made with good-for-you ingredients.

- Preheat oven to 350°F.
- In a mixing bowl, combine; brown sugar, egg, butter, and vanilla. Beat on medium speed until combined.
- In a separate bowl, whisk; almond flour, oats, salt, and baking soda. Whisk well.
- Add half of the flour mixture to the butter mixture, and mix. Once it is combined, add the remaining flour mixture, combine. Finally, add the chocolate chips and mix.
- Line a cookie tray with parchment or lightly grease it with non-stick spray.
- Scoop the cookie dough, about two tablespoons per cookie, and place a few inches apart. Roll the cookie into the shape of a ball and press cookie dough down using your hands or the bottom of a cup.
- Bake for 16 minutes.

Note

If you desire chocolate chip cookies always on deck, make a big batch of the dough, shape it into balls and freeze it. Then, when you need a sweet treat, just pre-heat the oven to 350°F., and bake for 18-21 minutes. This is perfect for moments when you only need a few fresh cookies.

Calories: 165 | Fat: 9 grams | Carbs: 15 grams | Protein: 3 grams | Fiber: 3 grams

Pumpkin spice chocolate chip muffins

1 box Spice cake mix
16 ounces Pumpkin puree
1/2 cup Applesauce, unsweetened
1/2 tablespoon Ground cinnamon
1 cup Chocolate chips

It is not officially fall in our home until I have made these muffins. They are easy to whip up and give you that cozy fall feel.

- Preheat oven to 350°F.
- In a mixing bowl, combine, pumpkin and applesauce.
- Next, mix in cake mix, cinnamon, and chocolate chips. (Be sure not to overmix, a few lumps are fine.)
- Line the muffin pan with muffin liners.
- Scoop 1/4 cup of batter into each liner.
- Bake for 20-25 minutes or until muffins have set.
- Remove from oven and cool.

Note

Use unsweetened canned pumpkin, be sure it's not pumpkin pie filling. These are great to freeze and save. Just bake, cool, and place in a sealed storage bag or container, freeze for up to 6 months.

Calories: 245 | Fat: 7 grams | Carbs: 43 grams | Protein: 2 grams| Fiber: 2 grams

Fudge brownies

¼ cup Water

1 tablespoon Instant espresso powder

15 ounce can Black beans, drained, rinsed

2 tablespoons Cocoa powder

1 cup Chocolate chips, melted

1 Egg

1 teaspoon Vanilla extract

1/2 cup Maple syrup

½ cup Almond butter

¼ cup Coconut oil, melted

1/4 teaspoon Salt

1/2 teaspoon Baking soda

Fudgy, indulgent, and delicious, just as it should be.

- Preheat oven to 350°F.
- Lightly grease an 8x8 pan.
- Warm water for :30 seconds. Then stir in espresso powder.
- In a blender or food processor, combine all ingredients. Whip it good!
- Blend until smooth and combined.
- Pour brownie batter into the baking pan and spread out evenly.
- Bake for 35-40 minutes.
- Allow to cool for 15 minutes before slicing into 16 servings.

Nutrition Note

The pureed black beans seem like a massive typo; however, they add the perfect fudgy texture, fiber, and protein.

Calories: 195 | Fat: 11 grams | Carbs: 22 grams | Protein: 5 grams | Fiber: 3 grams

Chocolate berry quesadilla
with almond butter

1 each Tortilla

3 each Strawberries, sliced

1 tablespoon Almond butter

1 tablespoon Chocolate chips

This dessert quesadilla is the perfect quick treat. It's layered with sweet berries, indulgent chocolate, and creamy almond butter.

- In a small sauté pan, on medium heat, lightly spray with avocado oil.
- On half of the tortilla, spread almond butter, then place in the pan.
- Top the almond butter with sliced strawberries and chocolate chips.
- Close the tortilla over the fillings.
- Allow to sear for 2-3 minutes or until lightly toasted, flip and repeat the 2–3-minute sear.
- Remove from pan and cut into two pieces. Serve warm.

Note

Swap your favorite seasonal fruit for the berries to mix it up.

Calories: 125 | Fat: 8 grams | Carbs: 13 grams | Protein: 5 grams | Fiber: 3 grams

Red velvet cookie bars

with cream cheese frosting

2 Eggs
1 cup Brown sugar
½ cup Tahini
¼ cup Butter, unsalted, melted
2 teaspoons Vanilla extract
1 teaspoon Red food coloring
1 ¼ cups Almond flour, packed
½ cup Coconut flour
2 tablespoons Cocoa powder
½ teaspoon Baking powder
½ teaspoon Salt

Cream cheese frosting:
1/4 cup Heavy whipping cream
4 ounces Reduced fat cream cheese
1/2 cup Powdered sugar
1 teaspoon Vanilla extract

I am obsessed with all things red velvet. Between the gorgeous red and velvet cream cheese frosting, I swoon for it. Yet sometimes the idea of cupcakes or a 3 layered cake is overwhelming but this recipe is simple and tasty.

- Preheat oven to 350°F.
- In a large mixing bowl, combine wet ingredients; eggs, sugar, tahini, butter, vanilla extract, and red food coloring.
- In a separate bowl, combine dry ingredients; almond flour, coconut flour, cocoa powder, baking powder, and salt.
- Add wet mixture to dry mixture, in thirds, mixing in between each add-in.
- Mix just until combined.
- Lightly grease a 9x9 Pyrex pan, pour batter into pan, and smooth out.
- Bake at 350°F. for 18 minutes.

Cream cheese frosting

- In a large mixing bowl, add heavy whipping cream. Using an electric mixer, whip cream on high until soft peaks form. (About 2 minutes).
- In the same bowl, add softened cream cheese, powdered sugar, and vanilla extract.
- Whip just until combined. Be careful not to over-mix, over mixing will ruin the fluffy whipped cream consistency.

Nutrition Note

This recipe is healthier by introducing tahini as fat rather than only butter. Tahini is simply ground sesame seeds, creating a paste/sauce. You can purchase tahini at your local grocery store. Sesame seeds are a great source of selenium, copper, iron and vitamin B6. Healthier red velvet cookie bars? I'll take two!

Calories: 235 | Fat: 16 grams | Carbs: 22 grams | Protein: 5 grams | Fiber: 2 grams

Healthy chocolate pretzel cups

10 ounces Dates, pitted

3/4 cup Almonds, raw

½ cup Peanut butter, natural

1 tablespoon Vanilla extract

1/4 teaspoon Salt (plus more for garnish)

1 1/2 cups Chocolate chips

1 teaspoon Coconut oil

22 Mini salted pretzels

This no-bake treat is perfection. Think of it as an elevated peanut butter cup. The date and peanut butter crust create a caramel peanut butter flavor, layered with chocolate and topped with salted pretzels. Your taste buds will sing.

- In a food processor, add dates and almonds. Pulse until broken up and combined.
- Add peanut butter, vanilla, and salt. Process until the mixture is thoroughly combined. It will create a crumbly-sticky mix. Stop the food processor occasionally to stir the ingredients ensuring large chunks become incorporated.
- Using a muffin pan, add muffin liners. Then, press one tablespoon of date mixture (crust) into the bottom of the 22 slots.
- In a microwave-safe bowl, combine chocolate and coconut oil. Microwave at 30-second intervals, occasionally stirring until melted and smooth.
- Add one tablespoon of melted chocolate on top of each crust. Then, using the back of your tablespoon, spread it out evenly to cover the crust.
- Top each cup with 1-2 mini salted pretzels.
- Sprinkle each cup with a pinch of salt.
- Place the muffin pan in the refrigerator until the chocolate becomes firm, about 1-2 hours.
- Store in an airtight container for up to 7 days in the refrigerator.

Note

Keep these cups refrigerated, they will refrigerate for up to 3 weeks or freeze for up to 6 months, but who can keep them around for that long? I love taking these to events or sharing them with friends because they are crowd-pleasers, and travel well.

Calories: 150 | Fat: 8 grams | Carbs: 19 grams | Proteinr: 3 grams | Fiber: 2 grams

Seasonally sweet

Baking with the season's harvest is a great way to increase your treats' flavor, sweetness, and nutrition. These recipes are focused on highlighting some of Summer's most prized produce.

Oat crumble baked peaches

filled with raspberry jam

Ⓥ

Serves 12 - Serving 1/2 assembled peach

6 Peaches, halved
1/3 cup Raspberry jam

Crumble topping
1/3 cup Brown sugar, packed
2/3 cup All-purpose flour
½ cup Old fashion oats
1 teaspoon Cinnamon, ground
1/4 teaspoon Salt
6 tablespoons Butter, unsalted, softened

Peach cobbler, peach pie, peach streusel…. Let's shake things up; what about a baked peach in all its juicy glory topped with jam and a buttery oat crumble?

- Preheat oven to 375°F.
- In a large bowl, combine all oat crumble ingredients, using a fork.
- Remove pits from each peach.
- Fill each peach half with one tablespoon of raspberry jam.
- Top each peach with two tablespoons of crumble topping. Lightly press crumble topping to form over the peach.
- Lightly grease a sheet tray or line it with parchment paper. Place crumble-topped peaches onto a sheet tray. Bake for 12-14 minutes or until the crumble has become lightly golden.
- Remove from oven and serve warm.

Note
Serve with ice cream for a show-stopping summer treat.

Calories: 230 | Fat: 10 grams | Carbs: 36 grams | Protein: 3 grams | Fiber: 2 grams

Squeeze the day lemon bar

½ cup Sugar, granulated

6 tablespoons Butter, unsalted, softened

4 tablespoons Applesauce, unsweetened

1 teaspoon Vanilla extract

2 cups All-purpose flour

Lemon Curd Filling

3 Eggs

4 Egg whites (or 1/2 cup)

1 cup Sugar, granulated

2 each Lemons, zested

½ cup Lemon juice, fresh (~3 lemons)

6 tablespoons All-purpose flour

1 teaspoon Baking powder

½ teaspoon Salt

These are classic lemon bars with some simple healthy swaps. These bars feature a soft, buttery shortbread crust and a tangy sweet lemon curd filling.

Crust

- Preheat oven to 350°F.
- Line an 8x8 inch pan with parchment paper and lightly grease.
- Using a stand mixer using a paddle attattchment, beat ½ cup sugar, butter, applesauce, and vanilla extract on a medium speed until creamy.
- On a low speed, add flour. Mix until just combined.
- Gently press the mixture across the bottom of a greased 8X8 baking pan.
- Bake for 11 minutes. Remove from oven and cool; place in the fridge for at least 30 minutes.

Lemon Curd Filling

- In a mixing bowl, whisk all filling ingredients until combined. Place the bowl of lemon curd mixture in the refrigerator until the crust is cooled.
- Pour mixture over crust and bake for 25-27 minutes. Or until the center is still Jello-jiggly, yet the edges are set.
- Remove from oven, place in the fridge and cool for at least 4 hours.

Nutrition Note

Adding applesauce to the crust lowers the fat and calorie content but maintains an indulgent shortbread flavor. Traditionally, classic lemon bar recipes will contain double the amount of butter. Store these in the fridge for 7 days. Garnish with whipped cream or Italian meringue.

Calories: 190 | Fat: 5 grams | Carbs: 33 grams | Protein: 4 grams | Fiber: 0 grams

Raspberry & chocolate clafoutis

Serves 5 - Serving 1 assembled clafoutis

1/2 tablespoon Butter, unsalted
1/2 cup Half and half
1/2 cup 2% milk
1/4 cup + 1 tablespoon Sugar, granulated
2 Eggs
2 teaspoons Vanilla extract
1 teaspoon Orange zest
6 tablespoons Gluten Free All purpose flour
1/4 teaspoon Salt
1/2 cup Chocolate chips
6 ounces Raspberries, fresh

Clafoutis is a baked French dessert, traditionally made with black cherries and baked in a creamy sweet custard.

- Preheat oven to 425°F.
- Brush 5 (2-ounce) baking ramekins with melted butter. Lightly coat the ramekins with 1 tablespoon of granulated sugar, swirling the sugar, and removing excess.
- In a blender, combine the half-and-half, milk, sugar, eggs, vanilla, orange zest, and salt.
- Add the flour and blend until smooth.
- Let the clafouti batter stand at room temperature for 30 minutes.
- Pulse the batter and pour it into the dishes, about 1/3 cup per ramekin.
- Evenly divide the chocolate chips and raspberries in the ramekins. (About 3-5 berries and chocolate chips per ramekin.)
- Bake the clafoutis for 5 minutes. Then, reduce the oven temperature to 375°F. Bake for 15 more minutes until the top is lightly golden and the custard is just set.
- Let the clafoutis cool for 5 minutes. Serve warm.

Note

Swap out the raspberries for any seasonal fruit; figs, blueberries, strawberries, cherries, or peaches would also be a treat. Garnish your clafoutis with whipped cream or a light dusting of powdered sugar.

Calories: 185 | Fat: 9 grams | Carbs: 22 grams | Protein: 5 grams | Fiber: 3 grams

Berry bread pudding

Serves 12 - Serving 1/12

7 slices Bread, diced into cubes
5 cups Mixed berries, fresh
6 Eggs
2 cups Milk, 2%
1/2 cup Sweetener substitute
1 tablespoon Vanilla extract
1 teaspoon Salt
1 teaspoon Cinnamon
3 scoops Vanilla protein powder (90 grams)

Juicy berries, fluffy bread, baked in a sweet custard. Need I say more?

- Preheat oven to 350°F. Lightly grease a 13x9-inch baking dish. Add diced bread cubes and berries, and mix well. Spread bread and berries out evenly in the pan.
- In a separate bowl, combine the remaining ingredients: eggs, milk, sweetener, vanilla, salt, cinnamon, and protein powder. Whisk well.
- Pour egg mixture over bread and berries. Gently press bread and berries into the egg mixture.
- Cover and bake for 1 hour. Remove the cover and bake for 10 minutes. Bake until custard is set, yet a bit wobbly, and the edges of the bread have browned.

Note

Top with maple syrup for a sweet breakfast treat or with vanilla bean ice cream for a classic dessert. Of course, have fun and swap out different fruit if you'd like.

Calories: 165 | Fat: 4 grams | Carbs: 22 grams | Protein: 12 grams | Fiber: 6 grams

snack-spirations

"Snack'a'doodle-doo": The calling your snack makes for you when it's snack time. Those mid-day morsels can make or break your healthy day. This chapter comprises quick-to-assemble snacks, and snacks that can be prepped in advance and taken on the go. So avoid diving into that bag of chips and grab one of these healthy treats instead. All these tasty bites are whole food-based and 250 calories or less to support you as you slay your day.

Snacks to keep you on track

Appetizer worthy
Roasted balsamic blueberries & brie crostini
Whipped feta dip
Bangin' buffalo chicken dip
Spicy garlic edamame

Getting cozy
Berry and almond stuffed sweet potato
Apple pie snack bowl
Apple pie filling
Protein hot cocoa

Bliss bites
Chocolate & granola bliss bites
Cookie dough bites
Peanut butter, chocolate chip, & oat bites
Cake batter bites

 Vegetarian Vegan  Gluten Free Dairy Free

Appetizer worthy

All snacks are not created equally. These snacks are above most; they are so good you need to share them with your friends and family at parties and gatherings.

Roasted balsamic blueberries & brie crostini

Serves 12 - Serving 1 assembled crostini

1/2 each French baguette, sliced thin, cut into ~12 slices
11 ounces Fresh blueberries
2 tablespoons White balsamic vinegar
6 tablespoons Sugar, granulated
1 tablespoon Rosemary leaves, fresh
4 ounces Triple cream brie

Balsamic roasted blueberries become almost like jam once roasted, then placed on creamy brie and a slab of bread. The only downside to serving this at a party is that you have to share.

- Preheat oven to 350°F.
- In a small bowl, combine the blueberries, balsamic vinegar, sugar, and rosemary. Spread out on a rimmed baking sheet. This mixture will become sticky, to avoid scrubbing, line the pan with parchment paper.
- Roast blueberries for 13 minutes. Remove the berries from the oven and place the sliced baguette on the pan. Return the pan to the oven and bake for 2 more minutes. The berries should be popped open with juices running out, and the crostini should be lightly toasted.
- Top each toasted crostini with a slice of brie and a spoonful of blueberries.

Note

These can be served while the berries are still warm, or you can make the components ahead of time. The berries can be stored in the fridge for up to 7 days. If you aren't a big brie fan, swap it out for goat cheese, gouda, or parmesan. Additionally, swapping balsamic for white balsamic is a great alternative if white balsamic isn't available.

Calories: 80 | Fat: 3 grams | Carbs: 11 grams | Protein: 2 grams | Fiber: 0 grams

Whipped feta dip

(V) (GF)

with honey, pistachios, & cracked black pepper

Serves 5 - Serving 1/4 cup

4 ounces Feta cheese
4 ounces Cream cheese, softened
1 tablespoon Olive oil
1/2 teaspoon Garlic, minced
1/2 teaspoon Basil, dried
1/4 cup Honey
1 tablespoon Pistachios, chopped
1/2 teaspoon Ground black pepper

Look no further for your go-to dish to bring to parties, potlucks, and game nights. This dish is a crowd-pleaser, plus it looks and tastes so fancy! Yet, it's quick and simple to whip up.

- In a food processor, combine feta, cream cheese, and olive oil until cheese is well combined and smooth. Add basil and garlic, mixing well.
- Scoop cheese from the food processor onto a small plate or into a shallow bowl. Use a large spoon to create a well in the center of the cheese. Fill the well with honey. Garnish the well with pistachios and black pepper.

Note

Dip apples, endive, chicken sausage, crackers, celery, or pita in this show-stopping dip. Make ahead if you'd like, and store in the fridge for up to 7 days. P.S. leftover whipped feta dip makes for a good spread on sandwiches or wraps.

Calories: 220 | Protein: 5 grams | Carbs: 16 grams | Fat: 16 grams | Fiber: 0 grams

Bangin' buffalo chicken dip

Serves 16 - Serving 1/4 cup

24 ounces Cottage cheese, 4%
¾ cup Buffalo wing sauce
1 tablespoon Onion powder
1 tablespoon Garlic powder
8 ounces Chicken, cooked, shredded
½ cup Cheddar, shredded
1/4 cup Green onion, sliced

It doesn't have to be football season for you to whip this easy, tasty dip up! This dip is creamy, spicy, and so good. Dip it with carrots, celery, tortilla chips, or pita.

- Preheat oven to 400°F.
- In a food processor, combine; cottage cheese, buffalo wing sauce, onion powder, and garlic powder. Blend until smooth and combined.
- In a separate bowl, fold the cooked chicken with the cottage cheese mixture.
- Pour mixture into an 8X8 baking dish and top with cheddar cheese.
- Bake for 15-20 minutes, or until cheese is melted and dip is warmed. Garnish with green onion.

Nutrition Note

Buffalo chicken dip is typically made with ranch dressing, mayonnaise, or cream cheese as the base, it's mixed with more cheese, hot sauce, and some chicken. The pureed cottage cheese makes this dip creamy and thick yet bumps up the protein amount in each dip. You can keep coming back for more on this one!

Calories: 80 | Fat: 4 grams | Carbs: 2 grams | Protein: 9 grams | Fiber: 0 grams

Spicy garlic edamame

10 ounces Edamame, in the pod
4 tablespoons Soy sauce, low sodium
1 tablespoon Honey
1/2 teaspoon Red pepper flakes
1/2 Orange, zested
2 teaspoons Sesame oil
2 teaspoons Ginger, minced, fresh
2 teaspoons Garlic, minced, fresh

Edamame is already fun to eat; we are amping it up in this recipe. The steamed edamame is tossed with a caramelized honey-soy glaze and orange zest.

- If frozen, place the edamame in a microwave-safe bowl and heat the edamame for 2-3 minutes or until defrosted.
- In a small sauce pot, bring soy sauce, honey, red pepper flakes, and orange zest to a slow boil over medium heat.
- Continue to boil gently until sauce is reduced by half, about 5 to 6 minutes, the sauce should thicken.
- Meanwhile, heat a large non-stick skillet or wok over medium-high heat.
- Add the oil, garlic, and ginger, and sauté for 30 to 60 seconds.
- Add edamame and soy sauce mixture and toss to coat evenly.
- Toss and cook for an additional 2-3 minutes or until edamame is heated.

Nutrition Note

Edamame is rich in several vitamins and minerals and exceptionally high in vitamin K, folate, and protein, making it an excellent snack.

Calories: 100 | Fat: 5 grams | Carbs: 8 grams | Protein: 7 grams | Fiber: 5 grams

Getting cozy

A nice satisfying snack that you can curl up with and enjoy.

Berry & almond stuffed sweet potato

Serves 1 - Serving 1 assembled

1/2 Sweet potato, medium, roasted
1/4 cup Greek nonfat yogurt, vanilla
1/2 tablespoon Almond butter
1/4 cup Berries, frozen or fresh
1/2 teaspoon Chia seeds
1/2 tablespoon Granola

Roasted sweet potatoes are the perfect vessel for fruit, a drizzle of almond butter, yogurt, and a sprinkle of granola for crunch.

- On a halved roasted sweet potato, top it with Greek yogurt, an almond butter drizzle, berries, and chia seeds.
- If berries are frozen, microwave them for a few minutes to release the juices.

Nutrition Note

Sweet potatoes are a great source of potassium, vitamin C, and beta carotene, plus they are deliciously sweet. Get ahead by roasting multiple potatoes in the beginning of the week, and quickly toss this snack together. Freeze roasted sweet potatoes for up to 6 months, pull them out of the freezer, and place them in the fridge overnight to thaw, then stuff and enjoy.

Calories: 215 | Fat: 6 grams | Carbs: 29 grams | Protein: 11 grams | Fiber: 7 grams

Apple pie snack bowl

Serves 1 - Serving 1 assembled bowl

1/4 cup Apple pie filling
(see recipe page 140)
1/2 Cottage cheese, 4%
1/4 cup Granola

Such a simple toss-together snack. The apple pie filling truly tastes like an apple pie; paired with granola, it's a great treat.

- In a microwave-safe bowl, warm apple pie filling for 20 seconds.
- Serve with cottage cheese and granola.

Nutrition Note

The cottage cheese packs protein, while the apple filling and granola lend fiber and micronutrients. Swap in Greek yogurt if that's more your style.

Calories: 230 | Fat: 10 grams | Carbs: 25 grams | Protein: 14 grams | Fiber: 2 grams

Apple pie filling

Serves 5 - Serving 1/2 cup

¼ teaspoon Avocado oil
4 cups Apples, diced, skin-on
¼ teaspoon Salt
½ teaspoon Cloves, ground
½ teaspoon Nutmeg, ground
1 teaspoon Cinnamon, ground
1 tablespoon Maple syrup
¾ cup Water

Cornstarch slurry
1 tablespoon Cornstarch
2 tablespoons Water

Serve this apple pie filling on cottage cheese, waffles, or oatmeal. It's such a treat, it can go on almost anything.

- Preheat a medium saucepan to medium heat.
- Add oil, and allow to warm for about 10 seconds.
- Add diced apples. Sauté for 4-5 minutes.
- Add salt, spices, maple syrup, and water.
- Continue to cook on medium-low heat for 10-15 minutes, or until apples have softened. Stirring occasionally.
- Combine cornstarch and 2 tablespoons of water, and slowly add to the apples until it reaches desired thickness. Continue to cook for 2-3 more minutes.

Note

Swap pears, peaches, or plums to mix it up. Make a large batch of the Apple pie filling and enjoy it for up to 7 days from the fridge. Or freeze for up to 6 months.

Calories: 60 | Fat: 1 gram | Carbs: 15 grams | Protein: 0 grams | Fiber: 2 grams

Protein hot cocoa

topped with whipped cream

Ⓥ ⒼⒻ

1 cup Milk, 2%
2 tablespoons Cocoa powder
1/2 scoop Chocolate protein powder
   (15 grams)
Pinch Salt
Pinch Cinnamon
1 teaspoon Truvia
Whipped cream

Suppose you are looking for a late-night chocolaty snack that is good for you. Look no further; this hot cocoa is rich, indulgent, and packed with protein. Top it with a dollop of whipped cream and live your best life.

- Warm milk in the microwave or on the stovetop.
- Add all ingredients (except whipped cream) to a protein shaker bottle. Shake it up. (The shaker cup helps eliminate clumps and foam the milk mixture.)
- Pour hot cocoa into your favorite mug.
- Top with whipped cream.

Note

Use your favorite; almond milk, 2% milk, skim milk, or soy milk will work well in this recipe. When choosing a chocolate protein powder, whey will be the smoothest in flavor, and plant proteins may have more of a distinct flavor.

Calories: 200 | Fat: 7 grams | Carbs: 15 grams | Protein: 26 grams | Fiber: 5 grams

Bliss bites

These tasty, fun bites are the perfect in-between snack. Added protein and healthy fats give you the energy you need to keep you going throughout the day. Serve as a nice, sweet treat post-meal or an on the go snack. Make a large batch and freeze it for future ease.

Chocolate & granola bliss bites

Serves 22 - Serving 1 bliss bite

10 each Dates, pitted
1 cup Granola
2 tablespoons Dried cherries
2 tablespoons Water
1/4 cup Dark chocolate chips
1/4 cup Almonds
1 teaspoon Vanilla extract
1 teaspoon Salt
2 tablespoons Almond butter

These delicious chocolate bites are such a treat. They come together so quickly and are too good just to have one. They are layered with energy-dense ingredients to keep you going throughout your day.

- Preheat oven to 375°F.
- In a food processor, combine all ingredients. Pulse until coarsely chopped and the mixture begins to bind. If the mixture isn't binding, add 1-2 tablespoons of more water.
- Scoop 1 tablespoon of mixture and roll into a ball. Place on a lightly greased sheet tray.
- Bake for 15 minutes.

Note

Dried cherries aren't a must, if you don't have any available, substitute any dried fruit such as raisins, dried strawberries, dates, or apricots. Once these bites are formed and baked, allow them to cool, then store them in an airtight container in the fridge for up to two weeks, or freeze them for 6 months.

Calories: 65 | Fat: 2 grams | Carbs: 11 grams | Protein: 1 gram | Fiber: 1 gram

Cookie dough bites

Serves 32 - Serving 1 bliss bite

5 scoops Vanilla protein powder (150 grams)
½ cup Maple syrup
1 cup Peanut butter, natural
¼ cup Mini chocolate chips

No bake mini chocolate chip cookies with protein, does it get any better than that? Loaded with vanilla protein, each little bite packs a nice punch of protein. Building muscle has never tasted so good.

- Combine all ingredients in a mixing bowl.
- Mixture will be thick.
- Form into a tablespoon-sized ball. (If the mixture is too dry to hold the ball shape add water 1 teaspoon at a time until the dough firms up.)
- Store in refrigerator for up to 7 days or freeze for up to 6 months.

Note
Make a large batch of these bites and store in the fridge in an airtight container or freeze for up to 6 months.

Calories: 95 | Fat: 4 grams | Carbs: 8 | Protein: 5 grams | Fiber: 1 gram

Peanut butter, chocolate chip, & oat bites

Serves 25 - Serving 1 bliss bite

1 cup Old fashion oats
½ cup Chocolate chips, mini
½ cup Peanut butter, natural
1/3 cup Honey
1/3 cup Chia seeds
1 scoop Vanilla protein powder (150 grams)

This flavor combination is a classic with reason.

- In a medium-sized mixing bowl, combine all ingredients.
- Scoop 1/2-ounce portions and shape them into a bite-size ball.
- If the mixture is too dry to hold the ball shape, add 1 tablespoon of water at a time to help hold together the mixture.
- Store in the refrigerator.

Nutrition Note
These little bites are packed in nutrition. Adding chia seeds adds fiber and healthy omega-3 fatty acids, while the protein powder punches up the protein content.

Calories: 100 | Fat: 5 grams | Carbs: 12 grams | Protein: 3 grams | Fiber: 2 grams

Cake batter bites

with white chocolate chips & sprinkles

½ cup Agave
1 cup Cashew butter
1 tablespoon Almond extract
5 scoops Vanilla protein powder (150 grams)
¼ cup White chocolate chips, mini
¼ cup Sprinkles

Cake batter as a healthy snack? YES! These little bites are loaded with healthy fats from nut butter and satiating protein. The sprinkles and white chocolate are for the soul.

- Combine all wet ingredients in a mixing bowl: agave, cashew butter, and almond extract.
- Add the remaining ingredients to the dry ingredients. Mix well.
- Mixture will be thick.
- Form into 1-ounce balls. (If the mixture is too dry to hold the ball shape add water 1 teaspoon at a time, until the dough firms up. If the mixture is too wet, add 1 tablespoon of protein powder at a time.)

Note

If you can't get your hands on cashew butter, don't sweat it. Simply swap in almond butter or peanut butter. Once your cake batter bites are formed, store them in an airtight container in the fridge for up to two weeks or freeze them for 6 months.

Calories: 95 | Fat: 5 grams | Carbs: 10 grams | Protein: 4 grams | Fiber: 1 gram

index

The terms "wellness," "healthy," "diet," and "cleanse" all suggest eating less. I think we should flip the script in a culture where food restriction is celebrated. Let's dig into healthy, flavorful, colorful, bold food! Food is fuel, my friends, and food is ah-mazing! Proper nutrition can improve your sleep, mood, overall health, skin, and athletic performance, just to name a few benefits.

Eat well and satisfy your cravings with recipes like weekend fluffy pancakes, blueberry muffins, loaded burger salad, chicken enchilada sliders, crispy fish tacos, and german chocolate whoopie pies. This book is packed with nutritionally balanced recipes that satisfy your cravings and fill you up. All recipes help you stay on track with a lighter, healthier twist.

$34.99
ISBN 979-8-218-14175-2
53499>

9 798218 141752